Small Acreages

Also by Georgia Green Stamper

Butter in the Morning

You Can Go Anywhere

Small Acreages

NEW AND COLLECTED ESSAYS

Georgia Green Stamper

Shadelandhouse
MODERN PRESS

LEXINGTON, KENTUCKY

A Shadelandhouse Modern Press book

Small Acreages
New and Collected Essays

Permissions
Shadelandhouse Modern Press, LLC
P.O. Box 910913
Lexington, KY 40591

This book contains creative nonfiction personal essays that reflect the author's recollections
of experiences in her life. Some names and characteristics may have been changed, some
events have been compressed, and some dialogue has been recreated. To the extent any
trademarks, service marks, product names, or named features are used in this work, all are
assumed to be the property of their respective owners and are used only for reference. Use of
these terms does not imply endorsement.

Published in the United States of America by:
Shadelandhouse Modern Press, LLC
Lexington, Kentucky
smpbooks.com

First edition 2022

Shadelandhouse, Shadelandhouse Modern Press, and the colophon are trademarks of
Shadelandhouse Modern Press, LLC.

ISBN: 978-1-945049-25-5 (Paperback)
ISBN: 978-1-945049-26-2 (eBook)

Library of Congress Control Number: 2022930061

Wendell Berry, excerpt from "Men and Women in Search of Common Ground" from *The Art
of the Commonplace: The Agrarian Essays*. Copyright © 2002 by Wendell Berry. Reprinted with
the permission of The Permissions Company, LLC on behalf of Counterpoint Press,
counterpointpress.com.

Cover and book design: iota books
Cover art: "The Homeplace," Jana Kappeler
Author photograph: Ernie W. Stamper

Map "Georgia's Natlee World": David Lowe and Ernie W. Stamper

For Ami, who would not let me
stop writing when I grew weary,

and

for Ernie, who has ever,
always, helped me keep safe
our small acreages of the universe

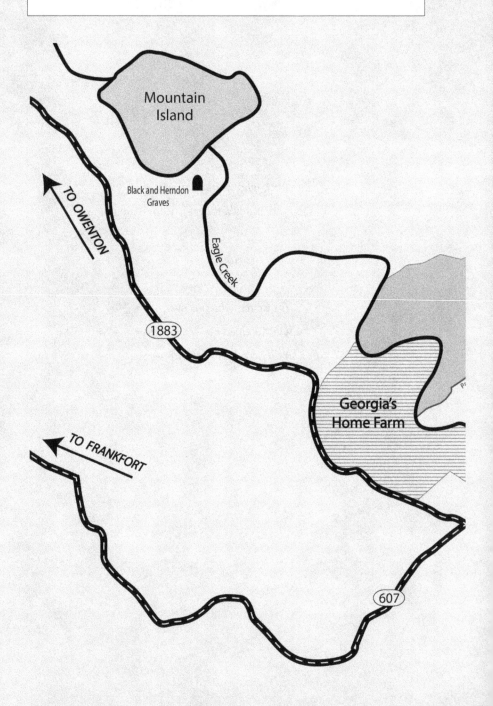

GEORGIA'S NATLEE WORLD

Mountain Island

Black and Herndon Graves

Eagle Creek

TO OWENTON

1883

TO FRANKFORT

Georgia's Home Farm

607

Location within Kentucky

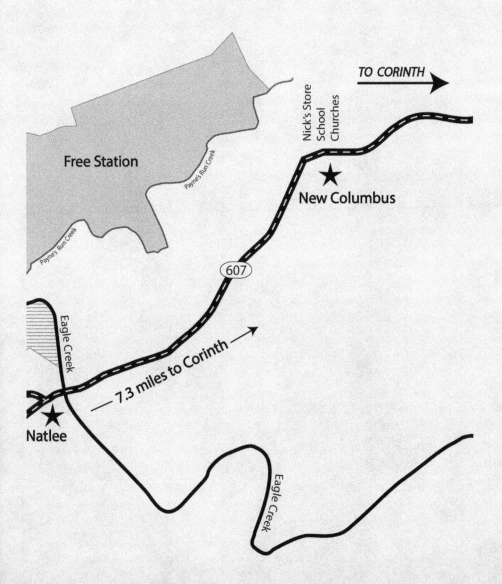

TO CORINTH

Nick's Store
School
Churches

Free Station

Payne's Run Creek

Payne's Run Creek

★
New Columbus

607

Eagle Creek

7.3 miles to Corinth →

★
Natlee

Eagle Creek

Contents

The Bit of Road That Lay in My View

Average Angels

My Small Acreages

INTRODUCTION

She opened her curtains, and looked out towards the bit of road that lay in view, with fields beyond outside the entrance-gates. On the road there was a man with a bundle on his back and a woman carrying her baby; in the field she could see figures moving—perhaps the shepherd with his dog. Far off in the bending sky was the pearly light; and she felt the largeness of the world and the manifold wakings of men to labor and endurance. She was a part of that involuntary, palpitating life, and could neither look out on it from her luxurious shelter as a mere spectator, nor hide her eyes in selfish complaining.

—George Eliot, *Middlemarch*

It may be that our marriages, kinships, friendships, neighborhoods, and all our forms and acts of homemaking are the rites by which we solemnize and enact our union with the universe. These ways are practical, proper, available to everybody, and they can provide for the safekeeping of the small acreages of the universe that have been entrusted to us.

—Wendell Berry,
The Art of the Commonplace: The Agrarian Essays

THESE LITTLE STORIES ARE MY REFLECTIONS on "the bit of road that lay in view" of my window on life and on "the small acreages of the universe that have been entrusted" to me. I hope only to add a handful of words to the ongoing conversation about what it means to be human. For me, what has made for a meaningful life has been defined by my relationships—between generations, with friends and kin, with the place I have known, its history, its weather, even with the culture as it has shifted around me.

The wise country people who raised me continue to remind me to pause and laugh at myself and the world in order to remain sane. I especially hear my father's sharp wit cutting through both the absurd and the awful, whittling it down to size, and my mother's admonition that "you might as well laugh" when life goes awry.

As I read through these stories again, I also am reminded of something my friend Jim said as he lay dying. Jim's passion in life had been music and singing in church choirs. And so it did not surprise his family when Jim said that a host of heavenly angels had surrounded his sickbed to sing for him. Visible only to him and heard only by him, the angels sang to him without ceasing in his final hour before death.

"What do they look like, Jim?" his wife asked, hoping to share in his glimpse of paradise.

"Oh, they're just your average angels," he replied.

This book, then, is dedicated to all the average angels I have known and to the bit of road and the hallowed smidge of the universe entrusted to them and to me for safekeeping.

Kinships

LOST AND FOUND

I'VE COME TO BELIEVE THAT LOVE, like light, keeps moving through time and space long after it leaves its point of origin. Sometimes I forget this. Sometimes, when it's dark—when my worries run wild—I think love is like sound, growing dimmer the farther it travels, until one day it vanishes from the universe. Then some little thing will happen, and I remember.

"SURE, YOU CAN TAKE THAT STUFF TO GOODWILL," my daughter said.

To be fair, she was in a hurry to get to work and I was only there to wait for a repairman. When you're in a rush, precision suffers. She waved in the direction of the pile of clutter in her garage but later would clarify that she meant only a particular box.

To be fair to me, well, in fairness, I don't come out looking good in this story. Excited by her permission to purge, I took advantage of her vagueness. Opened but unpacked boxes had been partially obstructing the path to her car since she had moved into the house four years earlier. A single mother with a demanding career, she has little time to deal with clutter in her garage. However, both she and I understand that she also is a hoarder like her granddaddy, my father.

Shan reminds me of my dad in other ways, too. Perhaps he loved this first grandchild so intensely that he imprinted her with his personality. Certainly he walked hundreds of miles "packing" her (as he phrased it) when she was a colicky, sleepless baby. She shares his kind heart, his intellect, and his passion for Kentucky basketball. She even laughs in the same loud, joyful, don't-care-who-hears-me way that he did.

But like him, she has a hard time letting anything go—even things she doesn't like and doesn't use. She recognizes this and tries to push back. She'd even started a box to take to Goodwill. I told myself she would appreciate my efforts to help her declutter.

I only had time that morning to empty two of her moving boxes, but the walkway in the garage looked better. I placed the newly unwrapped items on her kitchen counter to ask later where she wanted them stored. However, since she's short on space, I impulsively tossed a cheap glass bowl with painted flowers on it into her Goodwill box. Sort of tacky, it was out of sync with her taste and I'd never seen it displayed in any of her houses.

Late that afternoon, a violent storm slammed Lexington and plunged the city into a power outage that would last for over twenty-four hours. We were all unnerved, and Shan came over to sit in the darkness with her father and me. I filled the void chattering about what I'd gotten done that morning.

"You gave away a bowl with flowers on the sides? But Uncle Bo gave me that for my wedding!"

There was an edge in her voice that I'd never heard her use with me. I considered racing barefoot through the black night and smashing a window at Goodwill to retrieve the bowl.

Uncle Bo was Daddy's oldest brother, and they could have been mistaken for twins. Like Daddy, Uncle Bo was kind and loving. He also took seriously his responsibility as the oldest sibling in the Green clan of seven, even more so as first one and then another, including Daddy, preceded him in death.

He had just turned one hundred when my mother died. Yet he walked with me—on his walker—all the way to her January grave. Then, though I urged him to go home and rest, he insisted that two strong men carry him down the church basement steps to the fellowship hall. There, in the way of Kentucky kin, he would sit beside me as we continued our grieving over the traditional post-funeral meal prepared by the women of the church.

He was 101 when Shan married the next year. While he didn't dance at her wedding, he was there, looking sharp in his good dark suit, sound of mind, kissing the bride, laughing, and cracking jokes. He had a big time.

"Why would you take something to Goodwill without asking me? I only meant for you to take that one box." She was crying now.

It didn't look like the kind of bowl Uncle Bo would have given her, I tried to explain, but she broke in—

"He gave it to me with a note that said, *Since your Granddaddy is not here to give you this on your wedding day, I present you this crystal bowl on his behalf. Tap it and it will ring with the sound of his love.*"

Surrounded by darkness, we sat in a puddle of candlelight and cried. We cried because, in my effort to be helpful, I'd way overstepped adult boundaries. We cried because her Granddaddy and

Uncle Bo and all of those in that generation who loved us were gone. We cried because her marriage had not survived.

When our tears stopped, she hugged and forgave me. "What's a glass bowl between a mother and a daughter who love each other as we do?" she said. I could only nod and say, "Thank you."

In time, light filled our house again and Shan went home. She called the following night. "Mom, I unpacked more boxes and I found Uncle Bo's bowl!"

Since Uncle Bo had owned a glass factory in his prime, his gift, as I would have expected, was made of fine crystal etched with elegant flowers. I would never have casually tossed out such a beautiful piece.

I was left to ponder, however, the *what if*. What if I had sent it to Goodwill's bin never to be seen again? What if I—or my daughter— had broken it? What difference would it have made? Despite Uncle Bo's attempt at poetry, love, I remembered, is more like light than sound. It keeps moving through time and space long after it leaves its point of origin, nurturing one generation after another and random folk along its way.

OUR QUILTS

IN MAY OF 1949, OUR HOME EXPLODED in the middle of the night. No one ever knew why, although retrofitted wiring in the old farmhouse took the blame. When dawn came, we celebrated that we'd survived the inferno, yet the smell of smoke on our hair and skin was all that remained of our house and possessions. I was four years old, and my clear memory begins with the sense of having nothing left—no toys, no socks or shoes or underwear—only ashes of what had been, smoldering on the ground.

We still had the farm, which had been paid for a generation earlier, and the promise of the crop year ahead, but nothing else, no insurance, nothing. It's strange to begin again from nothing, particularly for a family who had lived on the same spot of land for more than a century. The reach for things that no longer exist goes on from habit. For years afterward, Mother would open a drawer to grab a this or a that and stop herself. "Oh," she'd say.

Our neighbors were tobacco farmers like us, and no one had much, but they shared what they could. Someone brought by a large meat platter that had belonged to her mother. It had a hairline crack but was still serviceable. Someone else gave us a Depression glass bowl from the dime store that Mother used for our Christmas salad for the next twenty years. Most people slipped us small, practical items—a kitchen paring knife or a dish towel. Cousin Debbie Jones, however, made us a quilt. It's the first one I remember.

I don't think Cousin Debbie was related to us, but one of her three dead husbands may have been, and so, in the way of our pocket of Kentucky, we called her Cousin. "I thought you all, maybe the girl, might could use this," she said in her almost-a-shout voice when she handed it to Mother after church. She would live until she was ninety-one, nearly deaf though independent to the end, but in the summer of 1949, when she made our quilt, she was not quite eighty.

Years later, I would run across a professor in college who repetitiously lectured on the nature of art, in the many classes I had with him at our small school. "Art," he insisted, "creates order out of chaos." I wish he could have met Cousin Debbie. She would have told him in her loudest voice that she'd been snatching order out of chaos all her life—in her pristine yard, her spotless house, her garden-fed table. And then she would have added, "Oh, and I quilt."

I would be dishonest, however, to imply that I saw Cousin Debbie as an artist when I was four years old. I claimed her quilt as my own because its worn-smooth cotton against my face helped me go to sleep on my new make-do folding cot. If it had a pattern, no one named it to me, but I do remember that I liked its many pretty colors, like Joseph's coat in the story I'd heard at Sunday School.

Sometimes it traveled from my cot to make a tent draped over chairs. As I got older and television arrived, I would roll up in it like a mummy on the floor to watch *Howdy Doody*, or I'd drag it out into the yard and spread it on the grass where I lay reading a book. By the time I left home for college, it was so ragged I didn't consider taking it with me.

Yet, on a weekend visit home during my collegiate years, I asked where it was. It would feel soft against my skin as I curled up in my girlhood bed again that night.

"Oh, I had to throw it away," Mother said. "It fell apart in the washing machine."

I guess I looked shocked because she went on, with a defensive edge in her voice.

"I thought you were supposed to use quilts. Nobody told me you were only supposed to look at them."

IN THE HANDFUL OF YEARS THAT FOLLOWED THAT CONVERSATION, I was busy finding my way in adulthood. I didn't give quilts another thought until my bridal shower. When I opened the last, large box, rainbow-colored squares arranged in interlocking circles against pure cream fabric spilled across my lap. Quilted with near-invisible strokes in the classic Wedding Ring pattern, the coverlet was a gift from my future mother-in-law. She'd made it the year she married, 1934, when the Great Depression still lingered over rural Kentucky.

The artistry of her exceptional needlework was lost on me—I don't sew at all—and as a farm girl dropped into the city, I was running from all things that spoke of country. As I passed it around the circle of admirers at the shower, I was worrying how I would make this heirloom blend with my Danish Modern bedroom furniture—the only style *House Beautiful* then deemed in good taste for sophisticated young couples.

WHEN MY MOTHER-IN-LAW DIED IN 1989, her will named me—the wife of her only child—the beneficiary of her "household goods." Those included five more quilts made by her and by my husband's late grandmother. Over the years, I'd seen them brought out for holidays and company-coming, to dress the beds and impress. Alone with them now, in grief, I saw them as if for the first time. How had my husband's grandmother, hit in middle age by Parkinson's disease, pushed herself to cut the squares, to thread the needle? Between tobacco field and kitchen, how had his farmwife mother found the time to create thousands of tiny stitches?

I touched the luscious colors with my fingertips. What stories hid behind each patch of fabric? Were the gold ones salvaged from the living room's wasted curtains when the crazed Kentucky River pushed the house from its foundation in the Great Flood of 1937? Were the pink pieces from a cherished dress? Had they bartered fresh-laid eggs at Mr. Thomas's general store for the red calico?

Their hardscrabble world had been ruled by a frugality so rigid it demanded the last inch of string be saved, each morsel of meat and produce consumed, every button hoarded until the collection exploded like popcorn from its keeping-box. If there would be art in their lives, I realized, function must justify it and thrift would demand it be squeezed from hoarded leftovers. I remembered my old professor's words, "order out of chaos." With their quilts, they had pushed back—as artists have always done—at the ceaseless ordinary, slipped grace into survival.

Now I was the last one who had touched their lives enough to care that they—not nameless women as anonymous as medieval artisans—had labored to bring these unique creations into the world. What would they have me do with them?

I remembered the joy I had taken as a child in Cousin Debbie's pretty quilt. I recalled that long-ago conversation with Mother when she'd defended our using it, because we needed it, until it raveled to threads. It had helped us piece together a new home when we had nothing. Now we were left with a new kind of nothing—all my husband's people gone but him.

That's when I made a decision not everyone will approve. I set about making my inherited quilts a part of our family's daily life, seeking a balance between the practical and the needs of the spirit. The most delicate, I've hung on the high walls of our house, like tapestries I've seen in European halls. A sturdier one I drape over an old table. The green and yellow Dutch Girl coverlet comes out whenever one of our six grandchildren stays overnight. And when I keep our youngest grandchild, I wrap her in the peach-and-blue baby quilt that my husband's grandmother made for him.

Two-year-old Georgia Jane has taken to that quilt like I did to Cousin Debbie's. She won't sleep at my house unless it's clutched between her hands. She doesn't know or care that she's napping on family history, much less on art. She's oblivious to the effort that went into its making, that her great-great-grandmother pushed trembling hands to create it.

Still, when Georgia Jane snuggles her face against the old cotton, I let reason fly. I fancy that she can see and hear the long-dead grandmothers as I do in my memory. They're giving us their approval, I decide, pleased that their work and love, like their DNA, continue to contribute to our family's story. Cousin Debbie joins the circle, too, and ever-deaf, even in my imagination, shouts, "Keep that child warm!" My mother slips in beside her and whispers, "Amen."

FAMILY REUNIONS

I WAS BORN INTO A SPRAWLING, indigenous-to-Kentucky, two-pronged clan, and each side of the family believes in reunions. We believe in the Constitution of the United States, too, but we would probably find something good to say about an anarchist if he were faithful at showing up at our annual potluck. In our view, attendance at these events is the cost of family membership and the dues would be cheap at twice the price.

My father's family has been gathering here and there on the first Sunday of August since about 1949. No one knows for sure what year we first met, but most agree that it was "after the war" and on the front lawn of my grandparents' farmhouse at the top of the Sparta hill. Uncle Bo, who lived to be nearly 102, recalled a few get-togethers with his cousins sometime in the late 1920s or early '30s. Over around New Liberty, he thought. But since there was a lengthy gap during the war years, and before and after, I finally persuaded him that we couldn't rightly claim that the annual reunion dated to the Hoover administration.

This side of the family laughs a lot and is fond of outdoor picnics and raucous games of Rook. During one golden decade, from the mid-'50s to the mid-'60s, Cousin Raymond hosted the annual shebang at his generously sized lodge at Lake Williamstown. He documented each of our get-togethers with his home movie camera. Although we look jerky and stiff in those old films, our smiles live on in color. These are silent movies, but as I watch them, I can hear the excitement in our voices as we anticipate riding in Cousin Raymond's grand motorboat. The boldest among us will give water skiing a try. And as always, the day will crescendo, after the Rook tournament ends, with a truckload of ice-cold watermelons.

We still view the Cousin Raymond era as the pinnacle of our reunion history. After his death, though, we persevered, and one relative after another stepped forward to organize and lead us. Now Uncle Bo's son, Bob, gathers us all to a park near Burlington. He spends the day cooking bratwurst on the grill, while yet another generation of children squeals and slides into a nearby muddy branch. Bob's counting on them to carry the family gatherings forward for another seventy years, I think, at least in their memories.

My mother's people hold the record for longevity, though. They've been meeting continuously on the Sunday before Labor Day since 1932. Being meticulous and organized by temperament, they have the recorded minutes and labeled, cataloged photograph albums to prove it. My mother, a child in bangs at that first reunion, grins at me across the decades from the squatting front row in the group picture.

Sense of place is important to this side of the family, and being talkers and storytellers, the Hudsons are partial to meeting indoors. Thus, for most of the past century, we've congregated at the old New Columbus schoolhouse in southeastern Owen County, where our people are from. Relatives routinely travel from all over the country for this to-do—from California, Louisiana, Missouri, Michigan—to eat fried chicken together in rural Kentucky, near Eagle Creek, the headwater of our family. We elect officers to pull us through the decades, sing hymns together, exchange genealogy charts, and conduct lively silent auctions to pump up the family cemetery fund.

Of course, the food can't be beat at these affairs. Someone always brings "old" country ham or scalloped oysters and Aunt Rose's corn spoonbread. My daddy's people roast fresh ears of corn in shucks on the grill. My mother's folks are long on green beans picked from the garden yesterday and cooked southern style until they give up and die in a puddle of grease. But reunions aren't about food.

They also aren't about extraordinary people—unless one believes as I do that ordinary people are extraordinary. We're out of work, on the move, on the way up, on the way down, getting sick, getting well, doing well, doing alright, getting born, getting to school, going after the American Dream.

Jim Henage, my cousin on Mother's side, likes to quote my daddy at reunion time. "A man has to be about fifty years old before he can appreciate his family," my daddy, Dexter Green, once told him. Jim says he thought that remark was odd—even silly—when he first heard it. He already loved his family, didn't he? But when he turned fifty himself, well, Jim says he began to understand what Daddy meant.

In the beginning, our reunions brought together somebody's grandchildren. Now the grandchildren are great-grandparents themselves, and we've forgotten exactly how we're related. The tie that binds us, though, is the shared journey through generations of time. The family is our unique slant on history.

COUSIN MAE AND THE HUDSON-JONES REUNION

NEXT SUNDAY, AS WE HAVE DONE EVERY LABOR DAY weekend since 1932, the descendants of Silas Hudson will meet for a potluck lunch in the village of New Columbus to reminisce. Not that anyone alive can remember Old Silas. He died in 1907. Although we've heard proud stories about his preaching and lawyering, in our opinion his sixteen children were his most remarkable accomplishments. With an admirable sense of fairness, he fathered eight with his first wife, Polina Abbott, and eight with his second, Zorelda White.

Of course, we don't remember his children either. The last one died in 1945. All of his grandchildren are dead, too. Their stories live on, however, in the scrapbook of photographs, newspaper clippings, and reunion minutes we've updated annually for nigh on a century.

The story of why a gathering of Silas Hudson's descendants is called the Hudson-*Jones* Reunion, however, is one that only I remember. It's not the kind of story, you see, that you run around repeating—"not outside of this house," as my grandfather would say—if you want to keep getting along with your kinfolks. That's not the way of our people. That wouldn't be polite. Still, it's a doggone shame, my mother insisted, that we've sat around eating together at a potluck for nearly a century completely confused about who we are, and according to my grandfather, George Hudson, it was all Cousin Mae Jones's fault.

Now, you need to understand that my grandfather, as he put it, "thought a lot of Cousin Mae." That's what my people say when they admire someone. (There's no need to get gushy.) Indeed, there was much to admire about Mae. She also was his wife's best friend, and she was married to one of his favorite cousins, Amos Jones. And even as he nursed his grudge against her in the matter of the conjoined Hudson-Jones Reunion, he rationalized her behavior. She was raised up in Canada, he reminded us. Before that, her folks had weathered life in Iceland, whereas the Hudsons had enjoyed the advantage of Kentucky's warmer winters for two hundred years. Maybe people of the Far North were bred to speak first and think later—before they froze to death—whereas we southern-born Hudsons had time enough to languidly amble toward the truth at an Emily Dickinson slant.

Yes, my family loved our Canadian cousin by marriage. I particularly appreciated her stories about her "best friend," which afforded me glimpses of the deceased grandmother I never met. Mae acted on Grandmother's behalf when she applauded any small success I achieved, and she genuinely celebrated my existence on earth. Had I been attentive, she would have taught me many things my grandmother may have hoped I'd learn.

She decorated her house, for example, with a sophisticated flair that eluded her country neighbors, and she shaped her ordinary yard into an English garden. A Julia Child in the kitchen before Julia even discovered butter, Cousin Mae was one of the finest cooks to ever stir a pot in Owen County. And always ready for unexpected guests, she set her abundant table with an elegance that would have made the Queen of England smile, had she dropped by Mae's at mealtime.

Although she excelled at all things domestic, her early ambition had been to become an opera singer. Not at the Nashville Opry we heard on the radio—but at the real one we knew little about. She'd been classically trained in voice in her Canadian youth, before Cousin Amos discovered her when he was working in Detroit. Love had led her back to his family's Kentucky tobacco farm where he was happiest. Now she stood not on a stage but beside the tin-tuned piano at our country church on Sunday mornings. She lifted her magnificent soprano voice to the heavens when we were buried. She sang at our weddings. She sang at mine. We appreciated her talent—but not enough.

She would live to be ninety-one, and until the end of her long life, I realize now, she remained a transplanted Northerner, always affable and trying to fit in, but not quite in tune with our Southern Kentucky ways. Too often she was unable to hear what we were *not* saying.

Thus, at the first official business meeting of Silas Hudson's descendants in 1932, Cousin Mae Jones stood up—pretty, blonde, and rouged—and made a motion to name our group "The Hudson-Jones Reunion." Now, this was not quite as outlandish as it might sound because several of Silas Hudson's daughters had married into the neighboring Jones family. Indeed, his oldest daughter, born in 1841 to his first wife Polina, had married a Jones, and by 1932, that daughter's progeny had been prolific.

As far as I know, first wife Polina's descendants and second wife Zorelda's were congenial. Yet in 1932 there lingered a polite divide between the two halves of Silas Hudson's clan. Perhaps Mae's intention was to bridge this gap. Who can say?

But for whatever reason, she—an in-law and a transplanted Kentuckian to boot shocked—Silas Hudson's talkative descendants into an uncommon silence. Those named Jones, possibly embarrassed, said nothing. Those named Hudson, definitely irked, said nothing either. Her outrageous motion carried without any discussion or a single nay.

To oppose it publicly, with Polina's and Zorelda's grandchildren sitting right there, eating fried chicken together, would not have been well-mannered. No, for the sake of politeness and accord that afternoon, my grandfather preferred to fume about Mae's motion until the end of his life, twenty-two years later.

I never heard him call our gathering anything other than "The Hudson Reunion" because, as he would explain, he didn't have a drop of Jones blood in him. It wasn't that he didn't admire the accomplishments of "those Joneses"—his cousins who became preachers and teachers and successful farmers and businesspeople. "It was the principle that mattered!" he would remind us. I'm not quite sure what the principle was, but I think it may have had something to do with DNA, which was not discovered until the year before he died.

After my grandfather's death, my mother took up his grudge, as any good Kentucky clanswoman would do. "People are getting confused about who we descend from! They are going on about a pioneer somebody named Tolliver Jones who has a million descendants! Why, we can't invite all his people in!" And so she would fret until the end of her life. By then, seventy-five years had passed since Cousin Mae thrust a hyphen onto Silas Hudson's descendants.

Last year, no one who attended our reunion was named either Hudson or Jones. Is that karma, I wonder, or only irony?

FATHER'S DAY 1954

THE LOBBY OF LEXINGTON'S OLD GOOD SAMARITAN HOSPITAL, fifty miles across the world from our farm, looked like a giant black-and-white checkerboard. Black, white, one step forward, two back. Gran Hudson was in the hospital once again. Father's Day 1954.

They would leave me there in the lobby on a hard, straight chair with a book because in those antiseptic days, children were not allowed in patients' rooms. A guard dog receptionist informed us with authority that no exceptions could be made.

I considered sneaking past her when she turned her head, but I was unsure what might happen once I passed through the portal to the sterile floors above. Would an alarm go off? Would the police come and haul me off to jail? Or worse, would they kick my grandfather out of the hospital, though, like Peter, I would deny I knew him?

Under the matron's watchful eyes, I feigned disinterest in darting up the stairs and with deliberate concentration stepped off the hours.

Third black square to third black square until I reached one hundred. White to white, black to black.

I would not become a nurse, I decided. I hated their silly little white hats that looked like the paper ones we folded in school. I hated their watchful eyes, on the lookout for a child hiding in a patient's room.

GRAN, MY PARENTS, AND I had lived together in a house on his farm from the day I came home as a newborn. I was his only grandchild, and he was my ever-present companion, an extension of who I was. Although he had been sick with an undiagnosed disease for a year, I didn't think of him as old. Tall, trim, and ramrod straight, his large personality and his stories filled our home with life and laughter. Wherever we went together in our little community, people respected him and were drawn to him and thus were drawn to me.

Mother was staying at the hospital with Gran now, sleeping in a chair by his bed. Daddy and I arrived at the hospital before noon. After he had checked in with Mother, he and I walked to the drugstore down the block for a sandwich. I was happy because this would give me an opportunity to buy Father's Day cards.

I spent a long time selecting the perfect ones, especially Gran's since he was sick. Finally, my choices made, I paid the salesgirl with the change I'd saved.

When we got back to the hospital, an odd thing happened. The receptionist looked at Daddy and without a word left her desk and walked slowly down the checkerboard hall to the ladies' room. The next thing I knew, Daddy took my hand and we started climbing up the stairs. No alarms went off. No one stopped us. I was giddy.

Gran was asleep when we walked in, and so I put his card on the table beside his bed. "He'll open it later," Mother said. When a nurse stopped by, I tried to shrink into a corner of the tiny room. To my surprise, however, she asked if I would like a Coke. Soon she returned with one poured over crushed ice. Was it possible I looked sixteen? I *was* tall for a nine-year-old.

The hours of the afternoon passed slowly in Gran's room. I thought about asking if I could return to the lobby, but that didn't seem like the right thing to do with the nurses so nice about my being where I shouldn't be. Gran woke a few times but didn't seem to know I was there. Then nurses started coming in every few minutes. Finally, they didn't leave.

About suppertime, Daddy said, "Maybe you could sit out there in the stairwell across the hall from Gran's room." And maybe I would count the stairs, I thought, top to bottom and back again, and say a prayer, and maybe then the nurses would make Gran okay.

After a while, Mother and Daddy came out and sat down with me on the steps. "Gran has died," one of them said, or maybe I just knew he had died without their saying anything.

It bothered me a lot that he hadn't seen my Father's Day card. Even then, I knew that was kind of silly on my part, a little thing, but I'd wanted to say those mushy things in the card and he didn't get to read them. Why couldn't he have lived another day, I wondered, or another week? It didn't seem fair for my grandfather to die on Father's Day.

If you had to die, I thought, you should die on an ordinary day, maybe when it's cold and raining and there's nothing else to do.

LEON HARRIS (1886–1960)

DR. JOHN GARST, PROFESSOR EMERITUS at the University of Georgia, contacted me by email:

> *I am doing research and writing a book on John Henry, the steel-driving man, a legendary figure in American folklore. In 1927, Leon Harris provided an important text of the song, "John Henry." In looking into Leon Harris' background, I find that he went from an orphanage in Cambridge, OH...to live with the Silas Hudson family, where he is found in the census of 1900....Do you know anything about all of this?*

"Well, yes," I replied. "Harris was mythic in our family stories. I even met him."

But where do I begin?

GREAT-AUNT LILY HUDSON, Silas Hudson's strong-willed, unmarried daughter, "got it in her head," they said, to take in an eight-year-old Black orphan to help with work in the house. An extra pair of hands in a rural nineteenth-century household that included her elderly parents and her bachelor brother would have been appealing. Most local people, however, seeking help in exchange for room and board, took in nearby poor white children.

Aunt Lily, though, was a devout and intelligent woman, influenced by the philanthropic movements of the late 1800s. Approaching thirty and childless, I suspect she emphasized her need for "help" to deflect criticism for taking in a Black child to raise. In the 1890s, the Civil War wasn't really over in Southern-leaning Owen County.

Lily's orphan turned out to be bright and personable and an eager student who delighted her father, Silas Hudson, a country lawyer and an ordained minister. The way my grandfather, George Hudson, told the story to me more than a half century later, Leon "was treated like a member of the family" in Silas's home. And Harris himself wrote that he was "treated like a white boy" by Silas Hudson. Defying local attitudes, Silas insisted that the child eat all his meals at the table with them, and on Sunday mornings, Aunt Lily ruffled feathers by seating the little boy beside her on the piano bench at the front of the Methodist church as she played for the congregation. "I need Leon to turn the pages of the hymnal," she said. I suspect she was protecting the child from being shoved out of a seat in the pews filled with her white neighbors.

Eighty-something Silas Hudson was so highly regarded in the community that no one dared challenge him directly for bringing a Black child into his family circle. But people criticized him behind his back, and a lifetime later, my grandfather was still defensive on *his* grandfather's behalf. In a distorted form of apology for Silas having defied local bigotry, Gran Hudson would boast with an in-their-face attitude about Leon's education, of his work as a well-paid railroader during the Depression, even of his writing poetry, though I suspect my grandfather never read a poem in his life.

Yet, when Harris came to visit our home in the summer of 1952, my grandfather did not invite him inside. He greeted him with warmth and courtesy at the door and then, after standing for a few minutes talking, asked him to sit with him on our wide front porch. In an era before air conditioning, we often sat with warm weather guests outside, and so this did not seem unusual to me. The two old men sat together for an hour or two, talking and laughing, enjoying each other.

Later that day, though, I overheard my mother criticize Gran Hudson, out of his hearing. She knew that he had been reluctant to invite a Black man into his home as a guest and had not uttered the automatic "Come in!" that was ingrained in our family's good manners. It's a glimpse of my kind grandfather at variance with all other images. I remind myself that he was born only a dozen years after the Civil War ended, that there were still segregated water fountains and restrooms at the Owen County Courthouse in 1952. Yet "Come in!" lingers unspoken, an unwelcome ghost haunting my memories.

I am indebted to John Garst for the rest of Harris's story. I have learned that his accomplishments were even greater than my grandfather realized. I understand, too, that Gran didn't have a clue how young Leon felt clinging to the outside of the only family he had.

According to Harris, most in the farm community—even some of Silas Hudson's family—kept him in "the n__ boy's world." He was happiest alone, in the woodshed, where he could hide and read, he says. He "ran away from the white folks" when he was rising fourteen, he writes, after a bad fight with one of Hudson's grandsons who taunted him. The fight didn't sit well with some of Silas's sons.

Walking and hitchhiking seventy-five miles, he arrived at Berea College, where he presented himself with a letter of recommendation from Aunt Lily, his "private teacher." He enrolled as a work-study student in the fall of 1900, but the infamous Day Law that would eventually prevail in closing integrated classrooms at Berea nudged him on to Booker T. Washington's Tuskegee Institute in Alabama by the fall of 1901. He studied there for three years and made influential friends. By 1915, he had been named to *Who's Who of the Colored Race*.

He worked at teaching, lecturing, farming, in steel mills, and for the railroad—"because he had to eat," he said—but writing was his passion, and he used that gift to encourage and assist his Black peers to reach for equality and a better life. He published numerous magazine articles and was editor and publisher of several Black newspapers. He was cofounder and president of the National Federation of Colored Farmers, active in the National Association for the Advancement of Colored People (NAACP) at the state and national level, served on President Hoover's Committee on Negro Housing, and corresponded with the likes of W.E.B. Du Bois, Martin Luther King Jr., and Thurgood Marshall. He published three volumes of poetry and, of course, collected and published an important version of the ballad "John Henry."

He also wrote an autobiographical novel, *Run, Zebra, Run*. A contemporary account of race relations at the turn of the last century, it has been discovered by academics and included in Black studies curricula. The cheapest copy I could locate on Alibris sold for $300, with some copies going for $600. So I rely on John Garst, who has read it, and on internet commentaries. It seems that Silas comes off well, but my great-great-grandmother did not. She's described as coming "from a... backward family... [who] aims to keep the 'little n__' in his place." Harris is graphic in his description of the verbal abuse and prejudices that his young, orphaned protagonist, "Leonard Hall," encounters in the household of "Silas Harker."

THE DAY AFTER LEON HARRIS VISITED OUR HOME IN 1952, he attended the Hudson-Jones Reunion. My father, Dexter Green, was presiding president that year, and he asked Leon to give the invocation. Harris responded with a prayer he said he had learned from old Silas. They were the same words I'd heard my grandfather, Gran Hudson, repeat at our table nearly every meal of my life.

> *Our Father, accept our thanks*
> *For these and our many blessings,*
> *Pardon and forgive our sins,*
> *And save us—*

UNCLE MURF

MY GREAT-UNCLE MURF HUDSON made the best brown sugar fudge I ever ate. He also cheated death on the Western Front in World War I, and decades after the war, he stood trial in Owen County, Kentucky, for attempted murder. My family didn't talk about any of that. And so I was a middle-aged woman before I learned that Uncle Murf's quiet, simple life on the farm had not been as quiet and simple as I assumed.

As a good-hearted and obedient boy who didn't mind hard work, Uncle Murf's youth was unremarkable. At age twenty-five, however, he became the archetypical American soldier in World War I. A farm boy who'd never been more than a hundred miles from home, drafted but patriotic, he was sent to fight the Kaiser in Europe. He did his duty without glory but also without complaint.

Though World War I did not officially end until June of 1919, when the Treaty of Versailles was signed, the fighting ceased in 1918 "in the eleventh hour of the eleventh day, of the eleventh month."

The "war to end all wars" was over, and the world exhaled and began to dance in celebration.

Except Uncle Murf. In a hospital somewhere in France, he lay waiting to die. He'd been gassed.

World War I, called our first "modern war," introduced chemical warfare to humankind. Alas, a modern battlefield death proved to be as hideous as the old-fashioned kind. Mustard gas, a slow and excruciating killer, took five weeks or longer to claim its victims. Giant blisters formed on the skin, inside the throat and lungs, in the genitalia, and in the stomach, where they caused hemorrhaging and vomiting. Blindness, severe headaches, a sensation of choking, and respiratory ills like pneumonia were typical. Those who did not die were physically compromised for life, subject to recurring respiratory ailments, especially tuberculosis.

By divine providence—or maybe by the infamous Hudson stubbornness—Uncle Murf survived. Still very ill, he was discharged on April 9, 1919. He was granted a military disability pension "for life," which the United States Army doctors assured him would not be very long—a matter of months, if not days.

He would live until 1989, two weeks shy of ninety-six.

To the army's credit, they continued to pay his disability check for the intervening seventy years. Late in his life, they even gave him an unexpected raise because someone noticed that he was drawing less than the lawful minimum.

In the decade or two after the war, he was often sick for long stretches. Over time, though, his respiratory ailments receded until he was bothered by no more than the occasional cold. Until the end of his life, however, he remained bone thin, a six-feet-tall arrangement of sharp angles.

Today somebody would write a book about his rehabilitation, call it *The Murphy Plan to Reclaim Health*. Uncle Murf, a quiet man, simply lit in doing what had to be done on the farm to survive, working any day he could walk. He kept at it until he was about ninety, hoisting tobacco upward into barn tiers, plowing, baling hay, whatever needed to be done.

He probably would have kept on until he dropped in the fields if his son had not insisted they sell the farm. By then, he agreed to quit, figuring he'd done well enough for a man with a seventh-grade education. He reminded himself that he'd bought a new Buick whenever he needed one, owned a brick house, owed a dollar to no one.

By the time I knew Uncle Murf, he was in his fifties, a kind, affable fixture at all our holidays, passing out his homemade brown sugar fudge. He always wore a near-new suit and tie, and when he arrived, his red hair was neatly held in place by a good-quality felt Stetson.

He was in his eighties before I had sense enough to ask him about his experience in the Great War. I could never get him to talk about his being gassed, though, or what it felt like to be drafted off an Owen County farm and shipped to Europe, which might as well have been the moon, I suspect, in 1917. All he would share were a few bits and pieces that amused him.

He would laugh out loud remembering their orders to put gas masks on their cavalry horses before they put them on themselves. The foolishness of saving horses before men still seemed ridiculous to him, a lifetime later.

He remembered that a well-to-do local businessman, J.A. Lee, gave a silver dollar to him and every Owen County soldier who left for the war from the Sparta train station. The largesse of that gift resonated through the decades to a frugal man like Uncle Murf.

And he told me about a pretty girl he'd courted briefly who tried to kiss him goodbye at the train station. "But I'd heard she'd gotten engaged to another man, and I wasn't about to get mixed up with her again." He chuckled, remembering her.

That was all I could ever pull from him about the war. Whether it was all he would let himself remember or all he thought I should hear, I cannot say.

However, I think that seeing "Paree" when he was twenty-five, as the song predicted, made him more adventuresome than his stay-at-home siblings. All I know is that my grandfather never went anywhere, while Uncle Murf and Aunt Bessie would climb into their Buick every few years to visit exotic-sounding places like California or Canada.

A steward in the Methodist Church, he was generous to the poor, sober, and ethical to a fault. But those who knew him well also knew not to push him. He had a peculiar temper, the out-of-nowhere kind that takes you by surprise. I wonder now if it could have been a form of post-traumatic stress related to his experiences in the war.

That brings us to the day that Uncle Murf shot an unarmed man. In fairness to Uncle Murf, the fellow outweighed him by a hundred pounds and had a reputation for being a bully. But even as I reconstruct the story, I have difficulty understanding how this disagreement escalated into a shooting.

It seems "Bully" had rented a house and lot that his landlord later sold to Uncle Murf. The sale required Bully to move out of the house, which he did, but for reasons lost to history, he left behind a huge woodpile. Uncle Murf—remember, he was ethical to a fault—would not burn or sell the wood because that would be stealing another man's property. Instead, he politely asked Bully, week after week, to remove it. Finally, he issued an ultimatum. "Move it by noon on Friday or else—"

The deadline passed with the woodpile untouched. As he'd said he would do, Uncle Murf confronted Bully at high noon. Like a scene in an old movie, the two men faced off in the lane. One step, then another, and another, Bully moved closer to Uncle Murf, taunting him as a fellow ready for a fight will do. Then, without a word, Uncle Murf went mad and his "or else" exploded. He pulled out a pistol no one knew he had and shot the unarmed man.

Fortunately—oh, thank God—Bully did not die, and a jury of his peers acquitted Uncle Murf of all charges. They cited Uncle Murf's good character and ruled that he'd acted in self-defense against a much larger man who had a reputation for being, well, a bully.

Mostly, though, I think they acquitted Uncle Murf because he was a World War I veteran who had managed to keep on living in spite of the Kaiser's best efforts to kill him.

THE DESSERT DISHES

LIKE OLD BONES, OLD DISHES CAN HIDE SECRETS in the earth for centuries until they're dug from the dirt, exposed, examined, and questioned. Other plates and bowls survive the passing of time intact, perched vain and proud on display where they prattle about their origins and net worth to any collectors who happen by.

My Great-Grandmother Hudson's dessert dishes—the five that survive—are neither silent nor boastful. Their past is no archeological mystery. In their heyday, they served up portions of Grandma's homemade cobblers to her Sunday dinner guests. They know they're pretty, with their cluster of pink roses circled by a scalloped border of gold filigree. But mass produced, they also know that they sell for only six dollars apiece on eBay.

For over two decades, my mother cherished these delicate bowls because the memories of her grandmother's family dinners—and of her grandmother—were dear to her. But there was another reason, too. Her Uncle Murf had asked her to take care of them.

Uncle Murf had bought them at his mother's estate sale in the late 1930s. Then one day, sometime in the 1970s, he arrived at Mother's door unannounced. He handed the dessert dishes to her wrapped in a dishtowel and told her they were hers to keep now. Variations of the story he told Mother have been repeated in countless other families.

By mutual agreement, Uncle Murf's son and daughter-in-law lived with him in his family home after their marriage. He appreciated their company and assistance since, by then, he was both elderly and widowed. Eventually, the young daughter-in-law would become an ex-daughter-in-law, however, and the dessert dish debacle may have foreshadowed the problems that lurked ahead.

The bride decided to freshen up the dated décor in Uncle Murf's house. Alas, her freshening process included the placement of her wedding china in the mahogany breakfront, which, in turn, required the displacement of Uncle Murf's antique glassware. In his version of this event, he came home one day and found his treasures, including his mother's fragile, rose-festooned bowls, plopped down on the garage's concrete floor, scattered here and there like pebbles on the beach. Others said the dishes were stored appropriately.

Regardless, his mother's prized dishes had been exiled and he decided it was time to pass them on to someone who would appreciate them. As he gave them to Mother, he told her something she did not know. "These were really Nora's."

Nora was his oldest sister, the second-born of the eight Hudson siblings. Nora's main claim to fame in our family lore was that she "stood six feet tall in her stocking feet," which was a remarkable height for a woman born in 1880. It was so remarkable that everyone who remembered her remarked on it every Memorial Day as we placed flowers on her grave. Since I shot up early, they speculated that I "took after Nora" and that I, too, might one day stand "six feet tall in my stocking feet."

Nora never married, and to my childish mind that seemed tragic. I worried that tall girls like Nora and me had trouble finding husbands. Not until I was an adult did I think to ask about the real tragedy of her life. Why did she die at the age of thirty-three years, one month, and twenty-three days?

"Well," Mother said, "I never knew her because she died in 1914, but I was told she worked as a nurse in the state tuberculosis hospital and ended up getting tuberculosis herself."

Now, sitting at my computer pulling up old records my mother never saw, I try to piece together more of Nora's story. In the 1900 census, at age twenty, she was living at home with her parents on their Owen County farm. Was she still waiting then for a suitor who would never come? Or was she always disinterested in marriage, eager to live an independent life?

How did this poor farm girl find her way into such an atypical job at the turn of the last century? Was there a shortage of people willing to touch patients with this dreaded disease? Did "standing six feet tall in her stocking feet" make Nora feel—or at least look— more invincible to the illness than others? My questions could not be answered. All I could learn for sure is that by 1906, Aunt Nora was living in Lexington where she was working as a nurse.

By the early 1900s, state-owned hospitals had sprung up to isolate tuberculosis patients and thus contain the spread of the disease. They also provided the patients with new treatments that were often successful. In Lexington and in Louisville, where she would later work, the new tuberculosis facilities were incorporated into the hospitals for the mentally ill that the state already operated.

It's an odd juxtaposition by today's standards, but it was a fiscally practical one at the turn of the twentieth century. And so Aunt Nora, full of hope, I presume, left home to work at the Eastern Kentucky Asylum for the Insane.

By the 1910 census, she had moved to Louisville's charming and prosperous semirural community of Anchorage, where she was employed at the Central Kentucky Asylum for the Insane. Her name begins to pop up in the *Courier-Journal* social notes, where she was listed as a frequent guest of a Mrs. Southward and other ladies. A nameless "colored man" rode her horse, Ping Pong, in a local horse show.

I suspect this is about the time Aunt Nora purchased her dainty bowls with the scalloped gold borders, perhaps at one of the fine stores on Louisville's Fourth Street. She had become a career woman with social connections and would have wanted to serve her friends dessert on appropriate china when they came calling.

But Nora's reach for an independent life would soon end. According to her death certificate, she became ill with tuberculosis in mid-1912. Despite her access to the most modern treatment of the time, her condition did not respond. She died on New Year's Day 1914, at her parents' Owen County home.

For precaution's sake, they would have burned all her clothing to kill the germs. But Great-Grandma Hudson kept her daughter's dessert dishes with the ornate pink roses. She would use them every Sunday until 1936, when she sold her home and moved in with her children.

IN 1995, MY MOTHER PRESENTED the little dishes to me on my birthday. I understood that the gift was meant to be a rite of passage, yet I've never quite been sure what to do with them. I tell myself that they aren't valuable, that they sell for only a few dollars apiece on eBay. Yet it doesn't seem right to serve ice cream to my grandchildren in gilt-edged bowls that are over one hundred years old.

But I keep them because I've learned that they do, after all, hide secrets, the interrupted dreams of an independent and brave young woman who stood "six feet tall in her stocking feet."

I keep them because it is my turn to keep them.

I'D GIVE A HUNDRED DOLLARS

MY DAUGHTER AND I WERE FIVE HOURS INTO A ROAD TRIP with two bored grandchildren in the back seat. They'd exhausted the usual diversions and had sunk to the level of bug-your-sibling-until-it-squeals. That's when I pulled out an old compact disc of Tom T. Hall's greatest hits, that I keep in my car. I was first drawn to Hall's music out of curiosity because he was born and raised in the northeastern chunk of Kentucky that became home to me in adulthood. I became a lifelong fan when I realized that he was a storytelling genius.

The thirteen-year-old, however, began to gag. Inspired by her humor, the nine-year-old joined in with noises only a boy can make. I restrained myself from giving them my opinion of current pop music. Every new generation celebrates its own, I understand.

But I didn't turn off Tom T. I wanted the children to hear the stories that he skillfully weaves into his songs. My favorite, "The Year That Clayton Delaney Died," is about a talented but broken small-town guitarist who inspired the storyteller's early musical efforts.

Hall concludes the story with regret that Clayton Delaney didn't live to know that his protégé became a success.

"That's the line that makes your grandfather cry," I told the half-listening children as Hall moved through the verses about Clayton Delaney.

"Cry?"

"Why?" they asked.

Why.

THE STORY BEGINS WITH *THEIR* GRANDFATHER'S GRANDFATHER, I tell them, a man named Ernest Beverly. Ernest, in turn, was the son of a tenant farmer named Jim Beverly, who never owned an acre of his own land. Jim raised tobacco on other men's hillsides all his life. In the cardboard photo that survives, he's good-looking and trim, with a shock of brown hair and kind eyes. They say he was a good worker, devoted to his family and the Methodist Church, but he had no chance to go further than his plow would take him. He could read and write, but like many poor men born in nineteenth-century Kentucky, he had only three or so years of formal education.

However, his oldest son, the quiet one called Ernest, would go to college. Owen County native John Wesley Hughes had founded both Asbury (1890) and Kingswood (1906) to educate needy students like Jim Beverly's son. Ernest, an eager student, heard Hughes speak at a local Methodist church and saw his chance. Encouraged by his grandmother, he left home around 1912 to enroll at Kingswood, 120 miles away. He went despite his mother's objections to his "uppity notions" and her tears that begged him not to go, not to leave her.

He wouldn't be able to stay long enough to earn a degree, but his year or two at college changed him, as education will do when it takes hold. He returned home a history lover, a person who pondered big ideas, a poor man who dared dream he could travel to the Holy Land.

He also returned with a plan. He'd work the land as his father before him had done, but he'd own the farm—the best one he could find. Persistence and frugality, some might say deprivation, defined his working life. Ledgers he left behind account for his money to the single penny spent on candy for the baby, the dime he put in the collection plate at church. Over time, he accumulated enough dollars and credit to acquire a large parcel of land in the rich valley of the Kentucky River Basin.

When he died at eighty-two, he owned a beautiful, fertile farm that followed the river as far as his eye could see. He had no debts. He had savings in the small, local bank, where he served as a director on the board. A modest man who lived simply, he was generous to his family and church. He never realized his dream of walking in the Holy Land, one he held on to until the final years of his life, but this son of a tenant farmer was no longer dirt-poor.

My husband, Ernie, named for Ernest, grew up in his maternal grandfather's home, three generations living together in the way farm families often did back then. The only grandchild, Ernie attributes much that is positive in his life to his Pawpaw's example and loving attention. My husband's decision to leave their farm and follow his skill with numbers into the corporate business world hurt and puzzled his parents.

His grandfather, however, did not discourage him. Perhaps Pawpaw remembered his own grandmother's positive voice overriding his mother's tears when he left home a half century earlier to attend college. Perhaps he intuitively knew that his grandson's work with an oil company would take him, if not to Jerusalem, at least to the world of his beloved Bible, to Babylon, the Arabian Peninsula, and beyond.

On one of Ernie's last visits with his grandfather, they walked across the land, Pawpaw pointing out improvements to the barn, that season's tobacco crop. When Pawpaw tired, they stopped to rest on a little rise that gave them a view of the valley. They were still, listening to the sounds of the place, the birds, the cows, the humid hush of the river. Pawpaw broke the quiet.

"I'd give a hundred dollars if my daddy could see my farm."

THE LYRICS CAME ROUND AGAIN echoing the words that had fallen from Pawpaw Ernest's heart so long ago. The children squirmed in the back seat, impatient with both my story and Hall's. I turned off the CD and gave them permission to return to their iPads. Someday, Tom T. might succeed in pulling them into his song but not this afternoon. Someday, they might appreciate Ernest Beverly's story, too, and understand the magnitude of his accomplishment.

Then again, maybe they won't. They're not the children of a tenant farmer born in the nineteenth century. With their twenty-first-century ears, they may never hear his life's story clearly. It's hard to understand the past, though it trails behind us, shaping even our molecules, pulling us down or lifting us up.

I stared at the horizon where the endless interstate met the sky and vanished from sight like the future I cannot see. What would the children comprehend of their own Grandfather Ernie's life and of my life—or we of theirs? Each generation celebrates its own music, I reminded myself, as I slid Tom T. Hall's greatest hits back into its case.

THIS IS A CHRISTMAS STORY

THIS IS A CHRISTMAS STORY. Sort of. Or maybe it's about grumpy old men. Maybe it's even about the commercialism that we pretend to dislike at this time of year. I'm pretty sure, though, that it's about some kind of love.

Pawpaw Green, ninety-three years and six months old, reached down to tie his shoes on the morning of December 20, 1970, and quietly left us. His death took me by surprise. I had assumed he would live forever—or at least until he was a hundred—frying up bacon and eggs in his rambling old house and grumbling about arthritis and the state of the world. Certainly I had thought he would live through another Christmas, and my first response was mild irritation that he had not obliged me.

Nobody wants to begin the holidays with her grandfather's funeral, but I also felt guilty of neglect. In mid-November, my first pregnancy had ended prematurely. Seeking comfort, unwell and grieving, I made the three-hour trip home to my parents' Owen

County farm at Thanksgiving. However, I decided not to make the twenty-minute drive from the farm to Owenton to visit Pawpaw Green that weekend, even though I had not seen him since August. "I'm too tired," I told my father, "and I'll be with him in a few weeks at his annual Christmas party."

I could have added that a visit with Pawpaw was not always uplifting. For starters, he couldn't hear anything I said. He had a hearing aid but was too frugal to waste batteries on all but the most important conversations. These apparently did not include my chatter. It saved money if he left the batteries on the table by his chair and he did all the talking.

He could be prone to grousing, too, and his stories, well, I knew they were supposed to be funny because his stone-like face would crack into a smile and his wide shoulders would shake with laughter when he finished telling one. Still, I often didn't understand his ironic and finely honed humor. The long-dead hapless characters who'd populated his life didn't amuse me as much as they did him.

And, I rationalized, others would drop by that weekend to visit him. The father of seven adult children, his clan, if you counted in-laws, numbered over fifty by 1970. No, he wouldn't miss me.

I was too young to appreciate what a marvel he was, living independently in his two-story house, mowing his large lawn with a push mower, walking most days to the Courthouse Square to talk with other old men. His mind was keen, too. He read every word of the *Courier-Journal* each day and watched *Huntley-Brinkley* each night on TV. At the moment of his death, he was better informed about current events than I was.

I also had only the fuzziest notion of what it's like to live through history. What could I, a child of postwar America's prosperity, really know about the life of a man born in 1877? Pawpaw's father had fought in the Civil War for the losing side and returned home sick and defeated. He died when Pawpaw was eight years old. That summer, with his mother near destitute, Pawpaw began hiring out as a day laborer in the fields.

Hard farm work would define his life, and so would devotion to family. I doubt that he had the time or inclination to be a playful father or even an openly affectionate one, but he kept his seven children clothed and fed and out of trouble. They graduated from high school, and several went to college—an accomplishment for a man who had to drop out of school after the third grade.

I did understand that he had always loved Christmas. Maybe this was because the holiday coincided with the end of the tobacco crop cycle, and Pawpaw could take time to rest a while, or maybe it was because the sale of the tobacco in December put a little cash in his pockets. Maybe it was because he missed out on his own childhood.

Whatever the reasons, Pawpaw Green embraced the holiday. Always there was a homemade fruitcake, even in 1917 when my father was born on December 22 and Pawpaw had to make it himself. When his children were young, the holiday gifts were as Spartan as the times—a little candy and an orange in the stockings and one toy for each child. (I still have my father's Lincoln Logs and have been charged with keeping them sacred for the remainder of my life.)

By the time my memory begins, however, times, though not abundant, were better. At his Christmas party, Pawpaw now insisted on placing a wrapped, name-tagged gift under the tree for every member of his clan of more than fifty, oldest to youngest, including in-laws. Everyone protested this was too much for him to do. "Draw names with the rest of us," we said. But he would not be dissuaded.

He drafted his youngest child, my Aunt Helen, as his designated elf, and off they would go to the small-town county seat of Owenton in early December to do his shopping. He would sit in a chair at Zuckerman's department store, smoking his pipe, and Aunt Helen would dart around bringing items to him for approval. The clerks formed an assembly line to gift-wrap his mountain of packages. Then it was on to the dime store to buy a toy for each child in the family. Cars were bigger back then, but I still wonder how they stuffed in over fifty wrapped boxes for the trip home.

Pawpaw's funeral was on December 22, my father's fifty-third birthday. The family decided to go ahead as planned with the Green family gathering the following Sunday. Pawpaw, of course, already had his gifts bought and wrapped, so Aunt Helen put them under the tree as usual.

I fingered the tag, *To Georgia Dexter from Pawpaw*. It felt strange, unwrapping a present from your grandfather a few days after you'd buried him.

But it did feel like love. And I have remembered that feeling in the harried rush of each Christmas season afterward, though I've long since lost and forgotten the gift from Zuckerman's department store.

UNCLE JUNIOR

THIS IS A STORY ABOUT UNCLE JUNIOR and maybe about all the poor Kentucky boys that war has chewed up and spit back out. It's about Daddy, too, of course. And it's about what Robert Frost called "home"—where, when you have to go there, they have to take you in.

I will begin with the letter that Daddy pulled out of the mailbox one morning in January of 1960. Edged in airmail's telltale red and blue flags, the envelope had been postmarked in San Diego, California. Daddy, done with morning chores, was at the house watching for the mailman. More precisely, he was waiting for the morning newspaper that the rural carrier also delivered. The letter's arrival stunned him, but he properly left it unopened until Mother and I arrived home from school that afternoon. "Here's a surprise," he said as he handed it to her.

It was addressed to my grandmother—dead since 1944—at Rural Route 2, Corinth, Kentucky. Since our family had lived on the same patch of earth for over a century, it didn't seem odd that a letter would find its way to a long-dead person at such a vague address. What did seem odd was that a ghost had neatly handwritten his name in the left-hand corner of the envelope.

Uncle Junior hadn't communicated with anyone in our family since he was home on furlough in 1943. Over the years, the mystery of "what could have happened to Uncle Junior" engaged my family's imagination much as Amelia Earhart's fate had fascinated the American people. There'd been no telegram announcing his death, but still we feared the worst. If not dead, then maybe the war had driven him mad. Was he wandering around out there unable to remember us?

Uncle Junior, my grandmother's half brother, was a late-in-life baby born to a second wife. That circumstance of birth thrust him into the same generation as his half nieces and nephews. He and my mother, separated in age by only two years, grew up together, close as siblings.

In 1930, when he was eleven, Uncle Junior's mother died unexpectedly. His father, aging, twice widowed, and disengaged emotionally, struggled to maintain a home for them. The Depression years were desperate times for many Kentuckians. Still, Uncle Junior's father has not fared well in our family's lore. Somehow, though no one was specific, "we" thought he could have done better by Uncle Junior. What I know for sure is that my grandmother—Uncle Junior's half sister—slipped him all the food she could spare. A little bite for him to eat tomorrow, you know?

Indeed, Uncle Junior did act hungry. He would stab his fork into the last piece of fried chicken on Grandmother's platter and ask, "Does anyone else want this?"

He probably needed it because he grew into a tall, broad-shouldered teenager. A star on the football team at Georgetown's Garth High School, he had dreams of playing in college. But his dad died in 1939, and by June of 1940, Uncle Junior had drifted into the Marine Corps.

Bad luck followed him. Stationed at Pearl Harbor in 1941 when the Japanese attacked, the Marine Corps initially listed him as "presumed dead." My grandmother sent an item to *The Owenton News-Herald* asking for prayer. It worked. In the chaos of that nightmare, he was resurrected, located among the wounded. The Marine Corps patched him up and sent him back to fight the war.

On that 1943 furlough, he visited the family at the farm. "Junior, whatever happens, stay in touch with us," Mother whispered to him as they hugged and said goodbye. "I will," he promised.

And that was the last time anyone in the family heard from Uncle Junior until his letter arrived out of the blue in 1960. My grandmother died in 1944. Both of Uncle Junior's older half brothers died, too. With each passing year, the enigma of his fate grew.

Mother would point to the spot where she was standing in the yard when she begged him to stay in touch and would ask, "I wonder what has happened to him?" She considered contacting the military to help her locate him, but she wasn't sure how to initiate that. "And what if he doesn't want to be found? What if he's physically or mentally impaired? Or even in prison?"

Her questions prefaced childhood memories of their swimming in Eagle Creek together, playing Monopoly, and spending their last dime at the school carnival. She talked about his charm and his rugged good looks and laughed about the "last piece of chicken" anecdote. She would end her reminiscing, though, with an observation about how hard Junior had it when he was growing up.

Uncle Junior's letter offered no explanation for why he had vanished from our lives. He wrote only that he had retired from the

Marine Corps a week or so earlier and that he was in an awful hard place. He begged "the family" to lend him seventy-five dollars to tide him over until he found a job, and he pledged his "allegiance to God" that he would repay it as quickly as he could.

Mother went silent as she read the letter. A teenage poet by then, I fancied I heard her heart break. I saw pain on her face, but then— relief? At least he was alive.

Daddy was watching her, too. Cash flow and farm expenses continually collided, and in 1960, seventy-five dollars was significant money for them. Then, in a quiet voice, he said, "I'll go to the bank tomorrow and get a loan."

That's when I became indignant. "How dare he show up after decades asking for money we don't have? Send half, if you send anything. Or send fifty."

Daddy shook his head and looked at me across the years that separated us. "If he's had to ask us, he's desperate." In the end, Daddy sent a hundred dollars.

Uncle Junior did repay Daddy, and he never asked to borrow money again. A lifelong bachelor and restless stone, he would live another forty-two years in faraway places, but he'd call Mother a few times each year until he died. If he ever explained his long absence from our lives—or if she ever asked for an explanation—she didn't tell me. Some questions, I guess, are better left unspoken and unanswered.

AMERICA McGINNIS

WHEN I OPENED MY EMAIL ON MOTHER'S DAY MORNING, I was surprised to find a "holiday greeting" from, of all people, the search engine at Ancestry.com. I've pictured him as a C-3PO sort of robot hunkered in a lonely basement alcove of the National Archives. Previously, he had displayed no sense of humor—only earnestly answered my requests for old census records and land deeds. Now, out of the blue, he wanted to share "fun facts" about the mothers in my family tree.

To be honest, I'd never thought about my maternal ancestors generating any fun facts. Mine are a stiff-lipped bunch of old daguerreotypes. Had he run across their lost diaries in his database? I was intrigued and clicked on the tantalizing link.

For starters, C-3PO (I like to call him that) told me that over the past two hundred years, three-fourths of the women in my family were twenty-five or older when they first gave birth. This statistic stunned me. It's not exactly a fun fact, but it goes against the tide of history when women married early and died young.

Perhaps my maternal ancestors were dowdy, hard-to-marry-off daughters who hung around the paternal hearth until destiny delivered a desperate suitor. But I prefer to think they were choosy women, the kind who delayed marriage until the fullness of womanhood, maybe after teaching school a few years. From what I know of my own mother and her stories of her mother and maternal grandmother, I know I come from a line of self-confident women.

Grandmother, for example, despite the simplicity of her life as an Owen County farmer's wife, insisted it wouldn't faze her a bit to have the president of the United States come to dinner. Everyone understood she meant it, too, because she could charm a fence post if she tried and she was a legendary cook, to boot.

I've tried to picture FDR bumping down the gravel lane to her farmhouse for one of her Sunday soirees featuring free-range fried chicken, plucked from her feedlot, and her famous fluffy biscuits. I've wondered what they might have chatted about. He'd probably compliment her "maahvalus" meal and ask for seconds. She would have thanked the president for his New Deal.

She might also have told him how much she valued education, how she read everything she could put her hands on, and by the way, wouldn't a public library in every county in America be a good idea? She, herself, had pushed both her daughters off to college in Depression-riddled rural Kentucky, she'd tell him.

My maternal great-grandmother survives in family lore as the likely source of any gentility, ambition, and intelligence we might have inherited. She was also a sturdy saint who anchored the family in the harsh years of late nineteenth-century West Virginia. While her underpaid preacher husband sought to save souls, she performed daily miracles in the kitchen. Prayerfully, she fed her family abundantly, graciously, with nothing much.

While the grandmothers admired their husbands *in particular*, I suspect *in general* they were skeptical—as my mother and her cousins were—of the male gender's leadership skills. They'd never heard the word "feminist," and I have no evidence that they participated in the suffragette movement. Privately, however, they may have opined that women were holding the world together.

"A woman pays attention to the details and gets things done," perhaps they said as they wondered out loud how the universe bumbled along with men mostly in charge. Men, they observed, liked to talk about the big picture but were nonchalant about the mechanics of daily life.

The most startling fun fact C-3PO shared about my matriline, however, was that it begins in this country with a woman named America McGinnis. If my family name had been passed down from her, mother to mother, generation after generation, I would have been Georgia McGinnis, not Georgia Green!

Of course, he arbitrarily began with her rather than reaching back to nameless grandmothers across the ocean. But I like the notion of beginning my maternal line with a woman strong enough to get through life named America. Was she America every day or only when she was naughty? I wonder if she were teased in the one-room schoolyard about her grand name? Or was it as common as Mary in those early, verdant years of the republic when hope bubbled from the earth like spring water?

No paintings have survived of America McGinnis, so I am free to picture her in my own image, a Scotch-Irish girl, very pale, with reddish-blonde hair. Widowed at age thirty-four and left with a houseful of children to rear, she'd probably laugh at my high-falutin' rhetoric if I asked her how she would define her American Dream.

But surely America McGinnis had one—for her family to come here, for her to endure.

Was it achieved when she escaped servitude in another's kitchen and became matron of her own? Was it about walking on farmland that belonged to her people and not to others? Was it Jefferson's "pursuit of happiness"—that phrase that seems to encompass all the other freedoms?

What ambitions did she have for her daughters? A brick house with a Williamsburg Garden? Silk dresses and books to read? Or did she only dream that they would have enough to eat, live to adulthood, and survive childbirth themselves?

And how did my America feel about being unable to vote in her America? Did she chafe at the irony? Did she question the morality of slavery? Did she ever look up and ask *why?* Or was her American Dream about the freedom to dream things that never were and ask, as Robert Kennedy later would do, *why not?*

C-3PO could not answer my questions. When I pressed him, he gently reminded me that America has many mothers—and as many stories—and that I, Georgia McGinnis, am only one of America's many daughters.

CONVERSATIONS WITH MOTHER

YOU'LL THINK I'M CRAZY, but I talk to my mother most every day. She died fifteen years ago. Oh, I don't talk out loud—now *that* would be crazy—and, of course, I have to hold up both ends of the conversation. But it's pretty easy for me to improvise her half of the dialogue because Mother tended to repeat herself. Maybe that's because I was a slow learner.

I know that we did a lot of different things together over our shared lifetimes. We cleaned the house, cooked and ate a million meals, shopped for a gazillion new outfits. We took trips to every historical site within driving distance and to beaches and mountains and cities. We celebrated holidays and birthdays and graduations. But in my memory, it all blurs together into one long conversation.

We did talk in all the usual places, places so usual they sound cliché when I name them. But yes, we did talk while rocking on the front porch of our farmhouse on summer evenings. We did talk around the kitchen table while Mother, always pushing back at ill health, had "just one more cup of coffee to get going." We talked in hospitals and restaurants. We talked in the car as we went from here to there.

And we talked on the phone. Even now, I occasionally stop my hand from dialing her to share something wonderful about my babies or to ask her a question. Before email and texting, Mother and I lined the pockets of AT&T with pay-by-the-minute long-distance calls. In metered, costly words, Mother talked me through college, through my challenges as a young teacher, through my pregnancies and all the stages of motherhood that followed. The weekly calls became such a ritual, when I moved far from the farm, that one of my little girls, angry with me, stomped her foot and threatened to never call me on Saturday morning when she grew up!

The problems I have now as I navigate the last decades of my life are different than they were before. Mother's advice, however, remains constant.

"Do what you know in your heart is right, and then don't worry about what others say." That was the Golden Rule reframed in Mother-speak, and if you really, really, really follow it, complicated situations become a lot simpler to navigate.

When I find myself in a ludicrous situation, she reminds me that "you might as well laugh."

And she continues to push me, "If something is worth doing, it's worth doing right." And even more important to her, "Do the very best you can with what you have to do with." Actually, Mother thought not trying your best, however modest your best might be, was a sin, maybe the mythical "unpardonable sin" she'd heard old-time people ponder. She'd taken the New Testament's parable of the talents to heart. You weren't expected to do anything great—unless you could—but you were expected to do the very best that *you* could do with your one talent.

She called doing your best "pride," and it was a compliment—not one of the seven deadly vices. Pride caused her to reach for a college education when most of her rural, Depression-era friends married in their teens. Pride pushed her to maintain her modest home in pristine condition, spotless and carefully decorated. Pride kept her farmhouse lawn manicured like an English garden.

Pride pushed her to bathe first thing every morning, meticulously dress, and put on make-up and earrings, into the final weeks of her life in her mid-80s—through years when she could barely walk across the room. She kept her red hair tinted and styled until the end because, well, you can't stop "trying your best" just because you're dying. Good grief.

And my favorite, "No use sitting there crying. Crying never solved anything. Just figure out what to do now, what to do next." Mother was a pragmatist and had little patience with self-pity because, well, it wasn't practical. It didn't accomplish results. I, on the other hand, am prone to tears and whining. At least once a week, Mother still has to remind me to "just stop it, Georgia, and figure out what to do now."

Life had hit her hard many times. My grandmother had a massive stroke when Mother was eighteen and died when Mother was twenty-three. She and Daddy lost everything they owned in a house fire in her late twenties. In her early thirties, she carried two stillborn children to term, pregnancies that left her with lifelong high blood pressure and compromised kidneys. In her forties, she was diagnosed with advanced glaucoma and was told she would soon be blind. When she was sixty-nine, Daddy was killed in a bizarre farm accident, and she was alone for the last sixteen years of her life.

But when my aunt once observed that she felt sorry for Mother because of all the bad luck she'd had, Mother was stunned. "Why would she say that? I've had a wonderful life! A very happy life!"

Mother had learned how to focus on the management of problems, not on the problems themselves, and to enjoy what the Bible calls "life abundant." Now, life abundant did not mean a *large life*. Mother did not envy others what they had that she did not, and she cautioned me to do the same. She would call my attention instead to the beautiful flowers in her yard, the great movie she saw on TV last night, and, oh—let's go down that road we've never traveled before and see if it leads us to an ice cream cone at the Dairy Queen.

A few years after Mother died, a woman showed up at one of my talks. She was a former student of Mother's, she said, and she'd driven fifty miles to meet me. Before I got too puffed up, however, she went on to explain that she'd come to apologize to Mother. Yes, she knew Mother was dead, that's why she'd come to talk to me.

She'd been one of Mother's top high school physics students, but when she was a senior, she had been party to a prank in Mother's classroom. It was nothing malicious or destructive, but it disappointed Mother, and decades later the woman was still haunted with embarrassment. You see, she'd broken every piece of Mother's advice. She had not done what she knew in her heart was right but had listened instead to what others talked her into doing. She had not done the best she could do that day in class, and consequently her grade suffered. And here she was, decades later, still sort of crying about what couldn't be undone.

I thought a moment, considering what Mother would say. Then I gave her a little hug and said, "After all these years, you might as well laugh."

SUMMER OF DOUBTS

IN THIS ONE, GRANDDAUGHTER, YOU ARE ONE MONTH OLD, looking sleepy and fat as a sausage. My mother, your great-grandmother, is cradling you in her arms, staring at your face, memorizing it to carry with her into eternity. She will have surgery for ovarian cancer three days later, and within seven weeks we will bury her. In this photograph, though, she is still very much alive and dressed to the nines to meet you. Her red hair is styled, her lipstick in place, her clip-on earrings shining, her leopard-print jacket impeccable.

It's what people call a "sweet picture," the kind that gets pasted into baby books and family histories, but when I look at it, my emotions fight with each other. I love remembering that she got to hold you and see that you were okay, that she got to see your mother's excitement and know that she was okay, too. But the question I didn't dare ask at the time lingers on the edge of my heart, taunting me. Did I do enough for her while doing so much for you?

Your mommy had been on bed rest for three months before your birth because you tried to get yourself born way too early. Frankly, my dear, you worried us to death that summer, but I was even more worried about your mommy. My strong, sturdy girl, a family pillar since her childhood, seemed on the brink of hysteria. She was convinced that you were going to die, like her grandmother's stillborn babies had done, or perhaps even worse, that you'd be born months before your time, damaged in a near-unbearable way.

Week after week, I divided my time between your fragile mommy, who lived in a city two hours away from mine, and my mother, who was in some sort of rapid, unexplained decline, huddled in her apartment near me, down the road. For your mommy, I cooked meals and decorated your nursery to keep hope alive and helped her cope with complete bed rest in an antiquated old house with only one bathroom—and it on the second floor. Mostly, though, I tried to keep her laughing, tried to keep her from going crazy. The nights, especially, were long and scary, with your father, a frazzled young medical resident, working thirty-six-hour shifts.

I didn't neglect my mother. Your grandfather was there to check on her every day when I was gone, and I came home to take her to her near-weekly doctor visits. Something was wrong, she kept telling everyone, but, well, she would need tests, and those took time and scheduling and most of all me, and she would say, "You've got your hands full right now with the girl." "We'll wait and do the tests later," she said, "after the baby comes."

She fretted about you so in those months before your birth, willing to gamble with whatever time she may have had left for your healthy arrival into the world. Perhaps she bartered her own deal with God or with the Devil because you arrived healthy and robust, full term, on October 2, and we buried her on New Year's Day.

You're way too young to understand what it feels like to be wedged between two generations, balancing the lives of both in your heart, knowing that each needs you in ways they never had before. We did the tests, finally, less than a month after you were born. I tell myself it would have made no difference if we'd done them in July, but that's the question I can't answer. That's the question that won't go away.

SO WE HAVE THIS BEAUTIFUL PICTURE OF YOU in my mother's arms on the last good Saturday of her life. She would have surgery three days after the photograph was made and would never get dressed again. And we have you, our gentle, compassionate, beautiful, smart, oh-so-wonderful Annelise, born out of our summer of doubts, our season of love.

Forms and Acts
of Homemaking

A BLANK SLATE
Ashland 1967–68

IMAGINE TCHAIKOVSKY'S *1812 OVERTURE* interspersed with Joan Baez's "Where Have All the Flowers Gone." Then, every fifteen measures or so, toss in Jimi Hendrix's psychedelic "Purple Haze." That would be the soundtrack if a movie were made of my coming-of-age story. The year that stretched from mid-1967 to the fall of 1968 was a bewildering moment to step into full adulthood. On the other hand, I may have been the only person who was bewildered. Most everyone else seemed dead sure of everything.

In June of 1967, fresh out of college, newly married, and full of dreams, I moved to Ashland, Kentucky, to join my husband. He'd been working there for several months, caught up in the decade's excitement about the newness of computers and the science that made them function. I very much wanted to be married to him, but I didn't much want to live in Ashland, Kentucky.

Cincinnati, Louisville, or Lexington, each about fifty to seventy-five miles from Natlee, were about as far away as I could picture myself living in those days. If I were to move beyond those familiar cities, then I'd be willing to consider someplace exciting, I decided, someplace I'd heard of, like New York or Chicago or Washington, D.C. But his best job offer had come from Ashland Oil and Refining Company (later renamed Ashland, Inc.), and its corporate headquarters were located in this small city in Eastern Kentucky. I could teach high school English most anywhere in that era when there was still a baby-boom–driven shortage of teachers, so our decision was easily made.

Physically and metaphorically, however, Ashland was about as far from my family's Natlee farm as you could get and still live in the same state. An exhausting three-and-a-half-hour drive over a crooked, two-lane highway separated it from all the places and people I called home. And if Natlee and its surrounds resembled Mayberry, my new town was a microcosm of Pittsburgh. In the 1960s, Ashland was a vibrant industrial powerhouse that boasted the largest privately owned railroad yards (C&O) in the free world. Mr. Blazer's oil refinery, ARMCO's enormous steel mill, and multiple chemical and power plants provided high wages to union and management workers alike. Perched on the bank of the mighty Ohio River and hunkered against the mountains of West Virginia, Ashland was an odd juxtaposition of the Appalachian Mountain chain and the industrial Ohio River valley.

On our farm in the Outer Bluegrass, air pollution was something I'd only read about in TIME magazine. In Ashland, I could see the air I breathed—or, as the locals were quick to tell me, I could inhale the odor of good jobs. During the thirty years we would live there, new federal laws gradually would improve the air quality, bleaching it to a near-normal color, but in 1967, it was dishwater gray. On bad days, when the wind blew the wrong way at the moment the steel mill belched, the sky turned a rusty red. What didn't enter our lungs lingered on the exterior of our lives, our porch furniture, our windowsills.

The fog aggravated the air pollution. It hovered over the Ohio River and, boxed in by mountains, often didn't lift until late morning. I felt like I was walking the streets of London in an old black-and-white movie. In the Bluegrass region I had left, heavy fog had been an occasional occurrence, not a near-daily event.

Back home, I was the fifth generation of my family to live on our land. Everyone knew me, my family, and our history, and I theirs. In Ashland, I was a blank slate, a circumstance that some would welcome but that I found disconcerting. I tried too hard with strangers—the cashier at the supermarket, the teller at the bank—as though saying, you'd like me if you knew me or maybe if you knew my grandfather.

I was happy when my husband was home, but I would dissolve into tears each morning when he left for work. "Please don't let the neighbors see you crying," he'd say when he kissed me goodbye. There was a tender sadness in his voice that made me want to cry even more.

Soon I would rally and give myself a pep talk. "Get a grip," I'd tell myself. "Stop this crying and get up and make this empty apartment look like people who have some gumption live here."

I'd remind myself that life on a farm might be free of air pollution and good for the soul, but it was back-breaking work, and at the end of the year it was always a wing and prayer for my folks to meet expenses and start again. And that would all be okay, but I found farm work dull. I was always sneaking off to read a book when there was work to be done. Having lived the life from birth, I did not harbor the romantic notions of the 1960s back-to-the-good-earth hippie movement.

Still, I would take one more minute to remember home, to remember lying in my upstairs bedroom on a July morning with a gentle breeze drifting in through the window. A cow would be mooing somewhere. I would hear Mother downstairs in the kitchen, moving around, righting the house, righting our world. The beginning of the beginning of my day, the ironed cotton sheets still slick against my skin, the pillow soft under my cheek, and I would be happy because she was down there, in charge, and I was not yet an adult.

That was it, of course. I was homesick because Ashland required me to be an adult. All the time.

My morning weeping did stop before the end of the summer. On a tight budget, I wrestled the townhouse into a comfortable place for grown-ups to live. I started teaching, and I soon knew people all around town. Many of them became forever friends.

But if I'd stopped crying from homesickness in the morning, the challenges of teaching often sent me home in tears in the evening. In another year, I'd find my rhythm in the classroom, and I think I developed into a pretty good teacher. But that first year, I felt like a failure. Despite my passion for language, many of my students couldn't distinguish a sentence from a prepositional phrase (although they had perfected the science of propelling spitballs that stuck to the classroom's high ceiling). The guidance counselor, in a well-meaning effort to keep the football players eligible to play (they did win the state championship that year), had placed many of them in my public speaking class. It was difficult to know whether they were more shocked by my expectations of them or I more shocked by what they managed to say. Being the only adult in a room with adolescents for seven hours a day was more exhausting than I had imagined.

Through my husband's job, I glimpsed the corporate world for the first time. Although LBJ's War on Poverty had focused national media attention on nearby counties, the Appalachian town of Ashland where I'd landed was a place of money and sophisticated people who had traveled places I'd only read about. I didn't play golf or tennis or bridge. I'd never flown on an airplane much less on a private company jet. And I didn't have a mink coat. Other than New York City in December, I've never again seen as many mink coats as I did in Ashland in the winter of 1967–68.

IF I'D BEEN CATAPULTED INTO A STRANGE, new place, the larger world I had known and relied upon was changing, too, right before my eyes— on TV's nightly news. In places like Haight-Ashbury, thousands of young people gathered to celebrate getting high on drugs. I never understood why then, and I still do not now. I cried because I did not understand them.

The Vietnam War went from bad to worse with the North Viet- namese's Tet Offensive, and anti-war protesters wreaked havoc on college campuses and in the streets. A hundred thousand strong, they nearly shut down the 1968 Democratic National Convention. The war had exhausted me. I surrendered and stopped reading the weekly recap of battles and strategy in *TIME* magazine. I didn't love the war. How can you love any war but especially one where the enemy is a metaphoric domino threatening an "effect" if it falls? But I didn't hate it enough to burn down a college building. I also had a tinge of guilt—and relief. My husband's draft number had come up, but a broken leg in college that did not heal correctly, combined with a history of asthma, had given him a deferment. Bewildered and confused about how I should feel about the war, I watched it in my living room on the *Huntley-Brinkley* nightly news and cried.

Martin Luther King Jr. was assassinated while I was on the road with a group of my students at the state speech tournament. Every Black teenager on the speech team cried all night long. I sat and cried with them. It was all I knew to do.

Two months later, Robert F. Kennedy was murdered by a lone, crazed gunman, minutes after giving a speech in his campaign for president. By then, I was too numb to cry.

But then American astronauts circled the moon on the *Apollo 8* mission. From their vantage point on the moon, they took the now-iconic photograph of the earth rising. It's a picture, many have opined, that puts human life in perspective. Certainly it helped me see the irony in my angst over a short move from an Owen County farm to Ashland. Still, when the road signs keep getting moved, bewildering a person, the trip into adulthood can seem as far, as long, as traveling to the moon from the earth.

Over a half century later, I feel as distant from that young woman of 1967–68 as she did from the girl she had been. I write, I think, to visit them both.

I remind myself, too, whenever I am faced with yet another uncertain change, that I cried and cried and cried when we moved away from Ashland thirty years after we arrived.

LILACS AND SPIREA

I'M PRETTY SURE I GASPED. Maybe I only think I did, embellishing the memory, but a sight that unexpected can make you gasp, and I'm pretty sure I did.

We almost didn't stop by the farm that afternoon. I was tired. Early that morning, we'd driven to Cincinnati, where I'd given a lecture. We needed to get home to Lexington for an evening obligation. But my family's vacant homeplace is halfway between those two cities and only a few miles off the interstate. Ernie and I agreed we needed to check on it after a winter of neglect.

I'm hesitant to admit this, given that the four generations of my family who preceded me spent every season of their lives there. But it depresses me to go to the farm in the wintertime, and I avoid it. The land that sustained us sleeps naked in winter, every ugly flaw exposed, every tractor gash in the mud, every crumbling fence. The old house is cold.

But this was spring, not winter. I needed to check on things, I reminded myself, as we pulled into the driveway in front of the house.

That's when I gasped. The farmhouse could have danced in a Disney fairy tale or been sculpted in fondant and served as a wedding cake. The old lilac and spirea bushes, covered in lavender and ivory lace flowers, had reached the second-floor windowsill of my girlhood bedroom. They jostled with each other down the sides and across the back of the white clapboard house, veiling it in a million tiny blossoms. Only the black roof peeked out over the flowers.

The sight of the blooming house had silenced us. Now I said, "I'm glad we decided to stop." What inadequate words.

"Yes," Ernie said. Then, "I'd forgotten how pretty lilacs smell."

Yes, I nodded. Maybe like the first new day on earth, I thought.

MOTHER PLANTED THESE SHRUBS, tiny switches Aunt Bessie gave her, around 1952, several years after the big house burned. Uninsured, my family hastily rebuilt a smaller home on the site. Faded black-and-white photographs document Mother's stories of the discouragement she felt in those first years after the fire. The unpainted concrete block foundation rises from the ground six feet or more where the site slopes downhill, and in the rear it's exposed a full story high. There's no grass. Big rocks dislodged by the jackleg builder's bulldozer rest where he'd shoved them in a hurry to be done.

I would have whined (or run off to an easier life, which I did). But Mother kept at the job, slow and steady, determined to turn ours into a beautiful place. My father and grandfather helped when they could. A lifetime later, crippled by arthritis in her spine, Mother would speculate that it was the making of the yard that put her on the path to her wheelchair. She lugged the heavy rocks away. She coaxed grass to grow in hilltop clay. And Aunt Bessie gave her plant starts.

I don't know how one gives a spirea or lilac start to someone. I remember Friendship Bread that made the rounds when I was a young wife. Its ancient yeast starter had been passed from friend to friend, one fermented pinch at a time, leavening friendship and expanding waistlines through generations. My batch, however, flipped over in the back seat of my station wagon on the way home. I never got all of that historic dough washed out of the car's carpet.

Aunt Bessie, though, knew how to start and keep plants alive. The yard that surrounded her pretty brick house was a botanical laboratory. Everywhere there was a blooming this or that, a mammoth fern, a towering decorative grass, an exotic bulb, a prickly succulent. Her out-of-control shrubbery created dim caves beneath their branches for sleeping cats and children playing hide-and-seek. Weeping willow trees fit for Tarzan to swing from screened the road.

I always thought Aunt Bessie's exuberant garden, though disorganized, deserved to be preserved like those on great estates. It hasn't been. The last time I passed by, the lawn was empty of all but some half-dead grass, and her house had the shabby look of rental property.

I don't remember a young Aunt Bessie, though she never seemed old to me. She always wore circles of rouge on her cheeks, and her hair fluffed around her face in permed waves. As a teenager, she'd left the farm for the city's shops and streetcars. I never heard anyone mention what job she held. Perhaps she only lived with city relatives like young country women do in Jane Austin novels. But for the rest of her life, she loved Cincinnati.

Marriage to my grandfather's youngest brother, Murf Hudson, carried her back to the country. I wonder now if her passion for growing flowers and exotic plants was her way of coping with her exile from the city because I don't recall her using her green thumb to grow vegetables. Those were left to Uncle Murf. Or maybe her yard was a boastful way of saying to the world, "I've been somewhere." Whyever, it pleases me that her spirea and lilac bushes are still blooming on my farm, if not her lawn.

A QUICK SEARCH TURNED UP A GLASS JELLY JAR left behind in the old kitchen. With my make-do vase, I plunged into the caves under the shrubbery to pick a bouquet like I did when I was a kid. The flowering spirea branches, prickly despite their delicate bridal-veil illusion, scratched my arms. The lavender lilacs were as soft as silk against my nose.

"I'm glad we decided to stop," Ernie said as we left.

"Yes," I said, "me, too." I held my jelly jar of flowers steady between my knees all the way back to our house in Lexington.

HOMINY

HOMINY DOESN'T GET AROUND MUCH ANYMORE. I'm not talking about grits. That's anorexic hominy, dehydrated until it can slide into a size 2 dress. It dances with shrimp in gourmet restaurants and gets invited to elegant *Southern Living* breakfast buffets.

Canned hominy is a good old boy—tough and swollen big as your knuckle. It's cheap, too. When I was a kid, Mother would buy ten cans for a dollar on special at the Owenton Kroger. A child of the Great Depression, she used hominy to stretch our grocery budget, but it also was an early convenience food. When she needed a quick and filling side dish for supper after a day of teaching school, she would often heat up a can of hominy.

I never gave it much thought beyond the obligatory spoonful on my plate, until hominy became an unlikely player in my transition out of childhood into all that came after. But then, most such stories do involve the unlikely, I suppose.

I WAS ABOUT THIRTEEN ON THE OCTOBER SATURDAY that Mr. Rook came to help Daddy pick our corn. I recall that he was a smallish, wiry man, about my height. Time has blurred his features, but I remember his thick shock of dark hair and the sound of his deep, raspy voice.

Jock Wright, who owned the farm adjacent to ours and regularly traded work with Daddy, came to help, too. He brought along his son, Charlie. Jock was a kind, intelligent man of the earth who could have walked straight out of one of Wendell Berry's novels. He and his black twinkling eyes deserve their own story, but I mention him here because he would retell the story of this day for the rest of his long life.

In the never-spoken-of social strata of our rural world, I realize now that Mr. Rook was clinging to the bottom rung. In late middle age, he'd wandered into our small community without a vehicle and without a known history. Although no one had spotted her in public, his common-law wife had arrived with him and they had set up housekeeping in an abandoned farmhouse.

The long-vacant dwelling could not be seen from any road and was inaccessible by car. It lacked even electricity. However, the absentee landlord, his distant cousin, said Mr. Rook could live there rent-free. Mr. Rook hired out by the day, as he was doing for Daddy this Saturday, to get by.

In that patriarchal time, the job of cooking for workhands fell to the farmwives who were glad enough to be excused from field work to the kitchen. Feeding their workers well was a point of pride for local farm families and especially to my parents. So Mother had baked a cake the night before and had gotten up early to put a cured pork shoulder—something she called a "picnic ham"—into the oven.

Within minutes, however, she was back in bed, vomiting. She'd been felled by one of her "sick headaches," a migraine accompanied by extreme nausea. It was a genetic malady she shared with all her maternal relatives, and I thank God every day that her DNA didn't pass it on to me.

Between heaves, Mother mumbled instructions into her pillow. "You'll have to pull the meal together. You have the hot ham and the cake—" She stopped to vomit. "That might do. If you fix anything else, though, keep it simple and make plenty."

"Make plenty," was Mother's golden rule in the kitchen. But what? Panic seized me.

I'd completed a 4-H project in cooking but had only learned how to make a simple cake, which was not simple to make at all, and today I didn't even need a cake because Mother had already made one. That was about the extent of my cooking expertise, once you got beyond stirring up a pitcher of Kool-Aid.

Frantically, I surveyed our larder. We had a big jug of applesauce. I could open that and pour it into a bowl. And canned biscuits. But would that be enough for men who'd been working in the field since early morning? Then my eyes fell on the stacked tins of hominy.

With Mother's words in my ears, I began prying metal lids and dumping hominy into a stew pot. We had sixteen cans, and I opened them all. I added a dollop of bacon grease like I'd seen her do, some dashes of pepper, and while the ham baked, I simmered my "vegetable." (Despite its bath in lye, hominy starts out life as corn.)

The first time the hominy bowl was passed, the Wrights said, "No, thank you." I understood my vegetable was not their favorite. They ate some of everything else, however, and then pushed back from the Formica kitchen table with polite compliments.

But every time Daddy would say, "Can I get you anything else, Mr. Rook?" he would answer, "I'd take some more of that hominy, if you got it."

By the time they returned to the cornfield, Mr. Rook had polished off sixteen cans of hominy minus a scoop that Daddy had eaten. It didn't seem possible, even though we'd watched him eat it. We were left to assume that our neighbor Mr. Rook really was that hungry.

From the distance of sixty years, I still remember the pride I felt as I washed the dishes after feeding the workhands by myself for the first time. I still hear Mr. Rook's gravelly voice thanking me "for the mighty fine dinner" as he left for the cornfield.

But there was something more, something that made me uneasy, though I could not articulate it. Now I understand that in some immature way, I had glimpsed the gap that separated our farm home from Mr. Rook's, though they stood only a mile or so apart as the crow flies across the creek.

To the end of his life, Jock Wright would tease me about that day. "Got any hominy?" he'd ask and laugh. Then he would shake his head and say with astonishment, still, after decades, and with a hint of sadness, too, "I never seen a man eat as much hominy as Old Man Rook did."

SETTING A GOOD TABLE

ALL OF MY FAMILY WILL BE HOME ON THANKSGIVING DAY, our three girls and our sons-in-law, and our six grandchildren. I'm short four seats at the dining room table and will have to convince the youngest to eat out in the kitchen. The friendly ghosts I've invited demand places, too, so we're going to have a big crowd around the groaning board.

My grandmother's soufflé-like turkey dressing—the secret is to toss, not stir, the breadcrumbs and drippings—will, as always, be an honored guest. And, of course, when Grandmother's dressing is in attendance, Great-Aunt Bessie's story insists on coming, too. That's the one about the time she threw all the uncooked dressing out to the cats and started over from scratch when Aunt Elizabeth accidently stirred instead of tossed.

My mother's pretzel salad—really a dessert on the lam—will be here as it has every year since about 1970 when she first stumbled upon the recipe in *Kentucky Living Magazine*. My other grandmother's claim to fame, blackberry jam cake with caramel icing, will squeeze in somewhere, along with my Daddy's absolute must—"old" country ham. And my blue enamel roaster with the slightly bent lid, the one Ernie and I bought at Heck's discount store over forty years ago, will escort Tom Turkey to the table.

The ghost who takes up the most room, however, is my grandfather, George Hudson. It's his pride in setting a good table that pushes me to work myself into a frenzy, cooking outsize quantities of food that we can't possibly consume, and way too many dishes, each guest's favorite.

"Set a good table." That's a phrase so long out of fashion I feel compelled to explain that Gran rarely lifted a dish in his life. His wife and daughters did the cooking and serving. No, for Gran Hudson, setting a good table defined his ability to provide well for his family and guests. In his world, the quality and abundance of food at his table was a mark of both a man's success in life and his character.

I don't know if Gran ever went hungry, but he was born in 1878 when the deprivation of the Civil War still echoed in Kentucky's rural countryside. He worked through years when his tobacco crop sold for a penny a pound. Hunger—or its cousin "barely enough"— lurked around the corners of his life, threatening to ambush him if he made a false step.

Setting a good table was about more than satisfying hunger, though. It was about pride, a little ego maybe, but mostly satisfaction at being able to please those he loved and liked. No one, not even the unexpected drop-in visitor, ever left his home hungry or unimpressed by his hospitality.

"Won't you stay for supper?" he'd ask in a voice that convinced you nothing would please him more. Or passing the prime dish to a guest the third time, he'd say, "Have a little more. It'll go to waste if you don't."

Meat, and plenty of it, topped his list of must-haves—home-cured bacon, sausage, and aged hams pulled from their hooks in the smokehouse, turkeys plucked fresh from his feedlot, and tender frying chickens in season. The garden filled the table with a cornucopia of fresh vegetables, tomatoes, green beans, and corn on the cob, in the summertime, and later in the year, cushaw squashes, yams, and potatoes.

His house was surrounded by fruit trees, "the orchard," he called it, apple and plum and two magnificent pear trees that still bear fruit a century after they were planted. There was even a mulberry tree, hanging with berries straight out of the nursery rhyme. In season, fruit turned up in fine pies and cobblers. In off months, it filled the preserve jars and danced with my grandmother's light-as-air biscuits.

Oh, there would be cakes, too, made with the sugar and flour he carried home, and cornbread from the cornmeal. He would gather hickory nuts and black walnuts to flavor Grandmother's candy. And popcorn—he loved popcorn, dishpans full of it—and grew it on the farm, too.

Gran Hudson's goal was to set a good table every day of the week, not just at holidays. There were those in our community, however, who couldn't do what he did. They would come to his door, after dark, and call him out to ask for help. They never left without the money they needed to buy groceries for their families, "a loan," Gran said, understanding that a man who needed a handout didn't need to have it called that. During the year he lay dying, felled by a mysterious blood disorder, one man drove a hundred miles, from Owen County to Lexington and home again, to donate blood once a month. "Payback to George for keeping my children fed," was all he said when my mother tried to thank him.

Oddly, despite his insistence on abundance, Gran Hudson was not a big eater. He was a tall man without an ounce of extra flesh on his body. His passion for food was not about gluttony but about pride—perhaps better called "self-respect"—and about love.

And so I'll cook too much for our Thanksgiving as I always do. I'll fix everyone's favorite dishes because I can and because I want to please them. And maybe, just maybe, the memory of my Thanksgiving feast will set a good table for family not yet born, as Gran's continues to nourish mine today.

JAM CAKE

BACK IN THE DECADES WHEN I STILL HAD HOPE of becoming trim, I sometimes fantasized about the last meal served to people on death row. In movies, at least, the script allowed those scheduled for execution at midnight the choice of ordering anything they wanted to eat one final time. I know it's a stretch to envy someone about to be shoved into the electric chair. But when you've been dieting forever, the thought of ordering up any food you crave is better than counting sheep, when hunger pangs keep you awake, and you've used up every calorie, every point, every carb allotted to you until dawn.

If there were no tomorrow, what would I eat right now, I'd ask myself. Usually, I'd home in quickly on some forbidden food lurking in my kitchen, tempting me like the apple in the Garden of Eden. I admit, though, that an apple, even the plumpest, the reddest, never enticed me to overeat. Oh, no, had I been Eve, the Devil would have introduced original sin into the world with a blackberry jam cake slathered in brown sugar icing.

I've always suspected there's something in my DNA that makes it impossible for me to resist this sinful dessert. Sure enough, my research confirms that this confection originated in Central Kentucky way back at the beginning of time—or at least as early as the nineteenth century. My people invented blackberry jam cake!

It makes sense when you think about it. Blackberry bushes grew on their Kentucky hillsides like the weeds they are, and you had to do something with all that jam. And if you made it right, jam cake would keep moist and dense for several weeks.

Now, you had to make it right. The sugar and the flour had to be moistened and flavored with lots of black walnuts from last fall's gathering, and raisins, too, if you were lucky enough to have a few. And, of course, it all had to be sealed tight with caramel icing made with cow's butter and brown sugar. (Real Kentuckians pronounce that *kar' mel,* accent on the first syllable, not *care-a-melll.* Good grief.) But if you made it right—oh, if you made it right!—it was a day's labor that could be banked and then withdrawn when needed to delight the old aunts and uncles at the summer reunion or guests come to visit on a winter night.

In our home, it doubled as a special Christmas treat and Daddy's birthday cake because it was always ready to serve by his birthday on December 22. Daddy could have devoured the whole cake in a single sitting. Instead, he shared it with all who came and went, cutting the slices of sugary love thin and measured to make it last, still moist, still dense, through Christmas Day.

Though it defies reason, jam cake is unheard of north of the Ohio River (where they go on about persimmon pudding, of all things, and shoofly pie). Imposters have damaged its reputation to the east, west, and south of the Outer Bluegrass, ditching the blackberry for any old kind of jam—even jam without seeds—and tossing in dates and prunes. Some even commit heresy and add coconut and cream cheese to the icing! And no, it's not a spice cake, though it's full of spices. And no, it's not a hard, sickening lump of fruit cake, though it does contain nuts and raisins. And no, it's not quite candy, though the traditional topping is only a few boiled degrees removed from chewy caramels.

Then again, no one quite agrees on how much of what goes in it. When I was growing up, every housewife I knew in Owen County touted her own unique recipe. Sometimes they were loyal to one that had been passed down for generations. Others had done some tweaking, adding or subtracting a little flour, sugar, spices, or eggs. Some cooks were loyal to lard or to Crisco, others insisted on butter, still others cooking oil. Some made a two-layer cake, others piled theirs three layers high. Others took to baking it in tall, round pans with a hole in the middle. Still others preferred a rectangular metal pan that produced a simpler one-layer cake. And so I was not surprised when multiple recipes for jam cake were submitted to our family cookbook.

The most elusive recipe turned up unexpectedly in Aunt Neb's files when she died a few years ago at the age of ninety. I say unexpectedly because Aunt Neb was more famous for her fried chicken than she was for baking. Yet there it was in Aunt Neb's handwriting, "Anna Mae's Jam Cake."

Anna Mae was married to Daddy and Aunt Neb's first cousin, and over a long lifetime, her jam cake became legendary at our annual family reunions. Her version may not have been better than anyone else's. Maybe it was only her consistency in bringing it year after year that fed the myth. In my memory, however, because that's the way of legends, it was the best of the best. Adding to the mystique, a vague secrecy surrounded the recipe, and it would have been lost to posterity had Aunt Neb not wheedled it out of a reluctant-to-share Anna Mae and preserved it.

Unfortunately, neither Cousin Anna Mae nor Aunt Neb left instructions on how to mix the cake or how long to bake it. Like fragments of a treasure map, only the list of ingredients survives, with a note that it makes three 9-inch layers that should be baked at 350 degrees. From there, you're on your own. As for me, I'm stirring it up in my imagination for the finale of my finale.

Anna Mae's Jam Cake

3 eggs, beaten

⅔ cup cooking oil

1 cup brown or white sugar

1 cup blackberry jam

about 1 cup applesauce

½ cup dark corn syrup

2 teaspoons baking soda added to 1 cup buttermilk

3 cups sifted flour plus ½ teaspoon baking powder

2 teaspoons cinnamon

½–1 teaspoon allspice

½–1 teaspoon cloves

½–1 teaspoon nutmeg

1 teaspoon vanilla

1 teaspoon salt

1 cup raisins

½ cup nuts, preferably black walnuts

GOOD BUT NOT GREAT

HEROES, I'VE HEARD, ARE MADE, NOT BORN. I'd say the same about greatness. You have to be in the right place at the right time for your greatness to get noticed.

Take Emily Weinstein, the food editor for *The New York Times*. Not long ago, she wrote a long and serious article for the most widely read newspaper in the world about—are you ready for this?—toasting toast.

Now I know what bad toast is. It's burnt. But I was eager to read what distinguished Weinstein's recipe for great toast from the run-of-the-mill sort that pops up out of the Cuisinart. I have to measure every ounce of bread I eat, so I can't fool around with average toast.

First, she begins with sliced bread. (Sliced bread is a big part of her recipe because otherwise it won't fit into the toaster slot.) Most any old bread will do that tickles your taste buds, unless it's Wonder Bread. (She really, really hates fluffy Wonder Bread.) Then you freeze it. Frozen bread is her secret for toasting great toast. When you get hungry, you simply pull a couple of frozen slices out of the freezer and pop them into the toaster. Violà! A new "convenience food," she calls it. The greatest thing since, well, since sliced bread.

That's it. That's *The New York Times* food editor's dead serious recipe for great toast. Butter and jam optional. Apparently, hers was such a radical, new approach to toasting toast that hundreds of the newspaper's readers left enthusiastic comments online. Summarized, they all said, "This is a genius idea!"

Down here in Kentucky, my mother started freezing sliced bread as soon as she got a freezer. That would have been a Kenmore from Sears, sometime in the late 1950s. When you live twenty-five miles from the closest supermarket, you worry about running out of basics like bread and stock up when you get to the store. However, bread molds quickly when left on the counter, no matter how you wrap it, and Mother, a child of the Depression, was not one to waste food. The only practical way to keep a stash of bread on hand was to freeze it.

Now, Mother did make great toast. And she did this even though she didn't own a toaster until I was grown. Her secret was to spread her frozen bread with a lot of butter. After that, she arranged it on a cookie sheet and placed it a few inches under the broiler in our electric range. It's true that the underside did not get as toasted as the top side, but that was part of its greatness. A buttery crunch on top that gave way to buttery sop on the bottom—oh my, was it good.

I was still digesting the accolades that Weinstein received for her toast recipe when I ran across a "Hints from Heloise" article that promised a breakthrough way to clean a peanut butter jar. While Heloise is not exactly Martha Stewart—Heloise is into practical, not pretty and pretentious—her column is syndicated in over four hundred newspapers. (I didn't know there were still that many papers left in the country, but that's what her website says.) She gets a lot of respect from Google, when it comes to household cleaning tips.

In the interest of full disclosure, I should reveal that I don't save peanut butter jars anymore, and so I don't try to wash them. That may sound wasteful for a girl who was raised up at Natlee, but my life has become cluttered and saving plastic peanut butter jars had to go. To be honest, I never knew what to do with them when I did save them. Now, since one of our grandchildren has developed a severe peanut allergy, we only consume about one jar a year on the sly. We keep it hidden on a high shelf, and it's a lot of bother to eat without contaminating the kitchen.

But back to Heloise. Here's her tip for cleaning a peanut butter jar.

Fill it with warm water.
Add a squirt of liquid dish detergent.
Let it sit for an hour or so.
Rinse with warm water.

That's been my approach to cleaning dirty *everythings* for a lifetime. Once I even followed this protocol with a nasty turkey roaster. In a hurry to get Thanksgiving dinner on the table, I shoved it, stuck meat pieces, greasy detergent water, and all, into the basement storage room to soak. Then I forgot about it until spring. My husband tripped over it when he ventured down there in the dark looking for a hoe or something come May. We nearly divorced over that incident—the odor of rotten meat can strain the best of marriages.

I'm guessing that Heloise never left a dirty turkey roaster soaking for six months, though. And I do admit that I've been known to try and pass off Wonder Bread as great toast—albeit frozen as hard as a brickbat. Maybe that's why my newspaper column is not syndicated and theirs are. I'm reminded, too, of the McDonald brothers who got run over by Ray Kroc and the guy who invented the airplane before the Wright brothers. I may have been there first with my frozen bread and my squirt-and-soak attack on dirty dishes, but greatness has eluded me.

But maybe if I renamed my column, Georgia the Great. Whadda you think?

DECORATING WITH LOVE AND PHILODENDRON

OH, JANUARY. It sweeps the holiday glitter out of my house and leaves it looking as woebegone as Cinderella after midnight. Discouraged by its dingy latte look, I decided to flip through the newest editions of several home magazines to see if I could add some zing to my old rooms in the new year. I shouldn't have done that. A woman who can remember when avocado green wall-to-wall shag carpet was considered avant-garde is obviously too old to become trendy.

But I never learn. In my lifetime, I have obediently morphed from somber copper-tone appliances to happy harvest gold. I matured into chic white. Now, HGTV has convinced me that only cold stainless steel can do the kitchen's heavy work.

In the 1970s, I filled every square inch of our family room with a gigantic "playpen" sectional sofa (covered in velvet, of course). In the 1980s, I junked it and swathed our refined, new upholstered pieces in sophisticated mauve. (Remember mauve? It doesn't get around much anymore.)

In the 1990s, however, I began to push back a little. I snubbed hunter green walls in the den and painted them taupe (that's beige with an attitude). However, the in crowd tut-tutted at my timidity, and I'm still chafing from their disapproval. My taupe also bucked the red dining room phase that came later, and that did not add to my decorating reputation either. Now my taupe is resisting the gray fad but only because I'm too tired to repaint.

I mention my history to make it clear I'm no rube. I understand there are trends in decorating, as there are in clothing. *The Brady Bunch*'s orange Formica everything would look as out of place in a home today as Mike Brady's leisure suit. But who decides when a plant goes out of style? For that matter, who decided that plants are out of style?

Flipping through the latest issues of *House Beautiful* and *Veranda*, I noticed that plants have vanished but sticks have arrived. More accurately, sticks with green leaves still clinging to them appear to have been freshly whacked from the nearest tree and stuffed into huge vases. These tree branches are artfully arranged on massive kitchen counters and on credenzas in gargantuan foyers.

I can see that resorting to sticks with leaves would simplify plant care. You wouldn't have to worry about how to keep your own blood-sucking version of Audrey II alive. All you'd have to do is toss her in the garbage every few days with a *ha, ha, ha, see you never* attitude and replace her with a fresh tree branch.

But here in Kentucky in January, we are scarce on leafy branches. I could probably come up with some leafless sticks, but my naked curly willow appears to be as passé as my mother's philodendron.

Which brings me to philodendron. When was the last time you saw a *Southern Living* editor plop a pot of philodendron on a table?

It gets no love anymore, even though its name literally means "love tree." And goodness knows, what the world needs now is love, sweet love, there's just too little of—well, you know what I mean.

In South Florida, I've seen philodendron growing outside, knee-high, in carefree abandon like Tarzan and Jane. It can also bring tropical romance indoors. One of the prettiest hotel lobbies I ever saw was encircled by a living curtain of philodendron vines cascading like an Amazon waterfall from the sixth-floor balconies to the first. Philodendron brings the love inside your home, too, where it will thrive, even for the ignorant or the lazy.

My mother loved philodendron. She started out with a slip of a vine sometime in the 1950s, and pretty soon its lush, green leaves covered an entire wall of her living room. Rubber plants came and went out of vogue during the next few decades—they were so popular they merited a hit song—but Mother stuck with philodendron. Ficus and fig leaf trees and schefflera—I tried those when they were trendy, but invisible bugs murdered them. Ferns—they shed so much inside in the wintertime my vacuum cleaner gave up and died along with the ferns. Mother only shook her head and said, "I'm loyal to philodendron."

Oddly, I never gave Phil an audition in my home while Mother was alive. It was, after all, not on any decorator's list of approved plants. When she died, however, I couldn't bear to toss her much-loved vine in the trash. I trimmed it back and carried it home, where I placed it in an upstairs bathroom above what the builder grandly called a "garden tub." What that means in outdated subdivision-speak is that the tub has an awkward window above it and a wide shelf under the window.

That was fifteen years ago. I forget to water it for weeks at a time and only remember to give it a splash of plant food about once a year. I've never replaced its original smidge of dirt. Now in advanced old age, it's happily wandering all over the place up there, giving hope to geriatrics everywhere.

So I'm just saying, if you can't pull off the "whacked from a tree fresh branch" look, give old-fashioned philodendron a try. Maybe easy and loyal—maybe love, too—will become a trend.

SWEDISH DEATH CLEANING

WHEN HER ADULT CHILDREN GET ON HER NERVES, my friend Pat threatens never to clean out another closet. She'll just leave them to deal with her lifetime of clutter after she's gone, she says, and see how they like that! I thought of Pat when I read about the Swedes and their obsession with death cleaning. Apparently, the Swedes feel a moral obligation to empty their homes of all but the bare necessities before they die. Apparently, their adult children never get on their nerves.

The Swedes are vague, however, on how to juggle the timing of a good death clean with death itself. Start too late, and it seems to me that you could be too tired with the exertion of dying to get it done. Death, after all, usually demands that its physical toll be paid in advance.

Start too soon, and you could end up living the last half of your life like a monk in a monastery. Even worse (in my opinion), you might have to do the death cleaning three or four times before you die. After all, even the Swedes might backslide if they bumped into the Highway 127 Yard Sale.

I admit, though, that I think the Swedes have a point. In my attic, I have every paper I wrote in college and even the diary I kept in high school. Do I really want my children to read those after I die—before they pitch them? And who will want the linen napkins edged in gold that Cousin Mae gave me fifty years ago?

On the other hand, I might want to revisit the words of my youth some slow afternoon in my dotage. It's even possible that I'll yet become a famous writer, and my biographer will need these early glimpses into my mind. And you never know when an antique napkin might come in handy for something.

I think my conflict results from being reared in an interfaith family. Daddy believed that keeping everything made for a frugal—and thus virtuous—life. He came from a long line of people who never threw anything away. This may have been because they were poor, so everything was valuable or repurposed. At their worst, they teetered toward hoarding. (His Aunt Grace's house is a story unto itself.) At their best, they preserved important pieces of family history—photographs, letters, one-hundred-year-old scrapbooks with newspaper clippings, and artifacts.

Mother, a lifelong Methodist, believed as John Wesley did that cleanliness was next to godliness, and to her that included clutter. She would have felt right at home in Sweden. In one infamous tidying incident, she threw away the day's newspaper *and* a $26,000 government check, reimbursement for conservation projects throughout the county to the local soil conservation district that Daddy chaired.

Over time, they worked out compromises to coexist. He respected her need for a tidy house, and she found ways to accommodate his desire to save. For example, his old glass jars were stashed under the hen house, and broken furniture he hoped to refinish, but never did, found a place in the barn.

The magazines, however, are the most memorable example of the way they lived in religious harmony. An avid reader and history buff, Daddy had grown up without access to public libraries. (Oh how he would have loved the internet!) His subscriptions to news magazines became his personal archive of information, and he could not bring himself to dispose of a single issue.

Eventually, his collection outgrew the basement, making a trek to the washing machine down there treacherous. That's when Mother came up with the idea of storing the magazines in a deserted cottage on the back of the farm, and Daddy agreed.

The old house became his bucolic library. Like Mark Twain's blue jay who dropped nuts down a chimney until a whole cabin was full, Daddy began to pile printed words in the empty rooms where beds and rocking chairs had once stood. Uncatalogued, the stacks of magazines grew ever taller as the years passed, until they scraped the ceilings in careening towers.

Years after his death, a tornado took the roof off the old house, shredding the magazines in the process. Tiny scraps of paper were left scattered across the countryside like a new invasive crop of seedlings. I stared at the mess and knew my mother would be horrified, had she been alive to see it. Yet I also knew that in a few seasons the elements would dissolve the bits of paper and that they would be absorbed into the soil. I thought Daddy might like that image, of words and knowledge he'd preserved, slivers of *TIME* and *LIFE* replenishing the land. It was a type of performance art, I decided, or maybe a "found" poem.

My mother's silent voice, however, observed that a tornado sure was a hard way to get a death clean done.

THE RECIPE FOR A GREAT HAMBURGER

I OPENED THE WINDOW OF THE CAR, and Summer slipped in beside me. "I know him," I said when the air conditioner objected to our picking up a hitchhiker. I'd been following him, I could have explained, watching for glimpses of him through the windshield.

I had almost forgotten the smell of his cologne, one part fresh-cut bluegrass, one part humidity, one part—oh, I can't name it. Maybe heat, the kind you see rising up in a haze on the horizon? But now I remembered. The scent of summer before time ran away.

"Whadda you want to do tonight, kid?" Summer's voice was a retro mix of pop classics. Crickets and tree frogs and faraway car horns with a hint of Elvis.

Would he laugh if I said I wanted to roll down the sloping lawn after the dew has fallen, like I did when I was a kid?

Yes, he would. "Your back would go out and never return."

Then maybe my bare toes could taunt crawdads in Eagle Creek's shallow pools?

He laughed again. "No, they'd pinch you and set off a siege with gout." When did Summer get so health conscious, I wondered.

I didn't mention reading poetry out loud in the cool of the barn to callow cows who didn't care a hoot (or a moo) that the raven croaked, "Nevermore." Even I blush at that overdramatic 'tween memory, but it *was* good preparation for later teaching high school English students who didn't give a hoot (or a moo) about what the raven said either.

But maybe I could eat a good hamburger outside at twilight, one like Daddy used to cook in the backyard on our first charcoal grill?

Before Summer could add up a cholesterol count, I rushed on, giving him no chance to interrupt.

We got the grill, I'm pretty sure, by redeeming Top Value stamps (which were always yellow and should not be confused with the S&H Green Stamps advertised on TV that our local retailers didn't give away). They really were stamps, with glue on the back, and each one represented a bonus point earned on purchases we'd made. Because they could be exchanged for gifts that tantalized us in a full-color catalog, we hoarded them in a growing pile in the fruit bowl. When they became so unruly, they spilled over the dish like kudzu and spread over the tabletop, someone—usually me—was delegated the tedious task of pasting them into little booklets provided for that purpose.

Invariably, no matter how many pages of stamps I licked, we needed one more to get what we really wanted—a philosophical statement on the human condition, I suppose. Nevertheless, many of the nonessentials that made their way into our frugal farm home came from the Top Value folks. That's how we got the black metal grill with its round hood and stork-like legs.

In the 1950s, "grilling" in the backyard was trendy, and we reveled in this newfangled way to entertain. Aunt Helen, Uncle Louis, and Cousin Judy were frequent guests. So were our neighbors, the Hunters and the Wrights. And sometimes we invited the entire youth group from the Methodist church to come on over for supper.

Only Daddy could light the charcoal, a risky business that involved lighter fluid and matches. And only Daddy could tell when the exotic square briquettes of charcoal we bought in ten-pound bags were the right temperature to cook our burgers. You could not mistake red coals and flames for "ready." No, you wanted a shade of smoldering gray that arrived a minute before starvation and that only he could discern.

Daddy's hamburgers started out on the food chain as "baby beeves" he raised on our farm. (Oddly, I had no moral compunction about this, but then again, the cows did snub my poetry readings.) It was Mother, however, who shaped the thawed hamburger into fat patties that she salted and peppered with abandon. I don't recall her adding anything extra, but when you begin with good meat you don't need to.

At the last minute, she would slather butter on the buns and stick them on the grill to toast, an inspired touch that lifted Daddy's burgers to unprecedented culinary heights, he said. We probably had sliced tomatoes and corn on the cob, too. But I only remember the burgers on the buttery buns, tender, juicy, and succulent, hot off Daddy's grill, and eaten outside on a balmy country night.

In the 1960s, hamburger fast-food chains hit the country like tornadoes, dropping down here, here, and here, forever changing the landscape and our diets. I wish I could say I remember the first McDonald's hamburger I ate, but mostly what I recall about that 1960ish visit to their walk-up stand on Lexington's New Circle Road are their French fries. Their burgers, then and now, remain unremarkable, in my experience. And what's up with slapping sesame seeds on buns? They have no taste whatsoever and lodge in random places in the teeth and gut.

To be honest, I can't remember when I last ate a really good hamburger, although I've eaten every kind that exists—from the cheap fast-food varieties to the expensive, hooty-tooty sort. From time to time, we even try to recreate Daddy's burgers at home, although it's never balmy on our deck, only too hot or too cool. And our fancy gas grill can't do the job as well as that cheap Top Value charcoal model. Even when we butter the buns, our burgers turn out too dry or too raw.

"Why do you think that is?" I asked Summer, who had now sprawled all over the car.

He was quiet for a moment. Then, with a touch of melancholy Elvis in his voice, he said, "Maybe when time ran away, it took the recipe for good hamburgers with it."

ELEGY TO A DOUGHNUT

WHEN I COME TO THE END OF MY LIFE, I suspect I will regret not having eaten more doughnuts. I'm not talking about the tasteless ho-hum lumps that come out of a supermarket box. I mean the hallelujah kind, puffed full of joyful yeast. Baptized in bubbling grease. Sanctified in a glaze of sugar.

Last weekend, Ernie and I were on full-time grandparent duty that began after school on Friday and extended until late Sunday night. Maybe you're better grandparents than we are. Or maybe you've never had to entertain two little boys (ages ten and five) and one little girl (age eight) en masse for three whole days in a Kentucky winter. Try not to judge us.

By Sunday night, we were flat out of craft ideas and supplies, bored with puppet shows and Disney movies, and weary of board games. Even the state-of-the-art video Wii device on the big screen TV had lost its fascination. Casting about for anything to fill an hour or two, we stumbled upon the idea of taking them to Krispy Kreme to see how doughnuts are born. Despite the lack of vegetables and protein, we could call it supper, I reasoned, on the grounds that seeing how a bakery works was sort of educational. "And Krispy Kreme does sell milk, too," I said a couple of times.

Annelise, a picky eater, though polite in her persnickety-ness, was concerned that the pungent odor inside the bakery would make her sick. That had happened once, somewhere, she thought she remembered. After some discussion, we decided that she could hold her hoodie over her nose and breathe through her mouth if the aroma of hot doughnuts nauseated her.

Owen held out for McDonald's, mostly to be contrary, but he reminded me that he's "allergic to nuts, you know, and there might be some flying around at a bakery." I told him I was pretty sure that wouldn't be a problem but reminded him that I always carried his EpiPen with me just in case.

Five-year-old Hudson, the doughnut lover in the group, negotiated a compromise. "McDonald's tomorrow. Doughnuts tonight!" And so it was settled.

Now this is a fairly well-traveled trio. We've taken them to lots of fascinating places in their short lives—the Newport Aquarium, Disney World, and as recently as October to a musical on Broadway in New York City. To my surprise, however, I don't think I have seen them more joyful than they were at Krispy Kreme. From the moment they crossed the threshold, the yeasty, warm odor of the bakery seduced them. Even Annelise dropped the hoodie from her face and joined the boys, pressing their noses against the twenty-foot-wide viewing window located deep inside the shop. They watched transfixed as the white lumps of dough traveled on their special track, plopped into the boiling fat, to emerge on the other side, aborn in gorgeous goldenness.

Then, as if wrapping them in love, a sugary glaze rained gently down on the newly created treats.

WHEN I WAS GROWING UP, there were no such bakeries near our Owen County farm, but oh my, I can still taste the doughnuts of my childhood, homemade in Mother's kitchen. Our new electric range was equipped with a built-in deep fryer that she would fill with lard rendered from our farm's butchered hogs. After the grease melted, then boiled, she would drop heaping tablespoons of yeasty dough into the vat. The gooey balls would sink to the bottom, and I would briefly panic. But after a moment's hesitation, they would resurface and float, bobbing, until they were golden brown. When they were "just right," Mother would lift them carefully with a slotted spatula out of the scalding fat and drop them into a brown paper sack filled with powdered sugar. My job was to shake the bag, ever so gently, until the doughnuts turned white, coated in gummy sweetness. Then Daddy and I gobbled them all down while they were still hot because there was no such thing as leftover doughnuts, he said.

OUR GRANDCHILDREN BEGAN TO LAUGH and run from one end of the long Krispy Kreme viewing window to the other, cheering on the endless line of white globs in their journey toward completion. And they were singing...What? Was that the Hallelujah Chorus I heard?

Finally, we stepped up to the counter and purchased a boxful fresh out of the grease, then rushed to a table before our sweet babies could cool. Hudson ate three and wanted a fourth. Annelise, who had thought she didn't like doughnuts, ate one and a half. Owen, though still loyal to McDonald's, ate two and a half. Ernie and I joined in, too—but don't tell my Weight Watchers leader or my physician! Because sometimes, on a cold winter night, it takes a hot doughnut kind of supper to remind you what it's all about.

BEAMS

IN MAY OF 1968, MY HUSBAND AND I MOVED into our first house. Our monthly mortgage payments were $118.98—or, as my husband boasted to everyone, six dollars a month less than the rent we'd been paying on our apartment. We were amazed at our financial cleverness. J.P. Morgan, watch out!

We'd stumbled upon our little house on a street full of trees while visiting our friends, Pat and Dave Botdorf, who lived nearby. It had languished on the market for a year, Dave said, because it was a family-unfriendly two-bedroom. But since we didn't yet have children, he urged us to take a look at it. The owners had been transferred out of state. When the house didn't sell in a timely fashion, their employer had taken over ownership of the house and slashed the price. Now it was "a steal," Dave said. "Please consider it," Pat urged. "It would be fun being neighbors."

Since two bedrooms sounded like an abundance of space to us, we called the real estate agent and made an appointment to see it. I quickly understood why the house hadn't sold. It had been abused by the previous owners' bad taste. They'd painted the bedroom burnt orange and outlined all the other rooms in black enamel.

But the house had good bones. We were especially struck by the living room's beamed cathedral ceiling, a stylish novelty in the '60s. Elbow grease was in our DNA, after all, and with a little soap and water and some fresh paint, we'd have a home to be proud of. (Did I mention the giant oaks in the backyard and the dogwood out front?)

Of course, neither of us had ever done any painting, unless the porch chair I'd painted one summer counted. But how hard could it be? I was assigned the walls and the reachable woodwork. My husband would do the ceilings and all the high stuff. Off we trudged to Heck's discount store to purchase supplies.

We figured we could cover most of the decorating sins with Lucite Antique White. Still, we were just sick that the earlier occupants had slathered black paint on the beautiful wooden beams in our story-and-a-half living room. So, when my husband happened upon a three-step product in Heck's aisle 10 that promised to return painted wood to a natural stained look, he was elated.

When we got home, he set about jury-rigging the mile-high scaffolding he'd rented. It was a "to-be-assembled" pile of yellow metal pipes, odd little wheels, and a rickety-looking platform.

Then he explained the process to me. First, he would apply a flat brown undercoat to the beams, or maybe it would take two, he didn't know. Several days later, when it was fully dry, he'd apply a coat of stain, and then finally, a coat of shellac.

I was skeptical of this plan from the outset, but as the undercoat went on, my hesitation escalated to alarm. Human excrement—the color of diarrhea, to be precise—is the only thing that approximates this shade in nature. My husband kept assuring me that it would "look better once the other coats go on."

My parents came to town during this phase of the project. Daddy quietly opined to my mother and me that it looked like something Pap—his father, born shortly after the Civil War—might have done. I winced because Pap was notorious for his questionable home improvements. And, of course, I, too, remembered the story of how he'd gotten a deal sometime during the Great Depression on twenty gallons of paint in a color much like this one. Everything in his house, from the pine floors to the woodwork to porch furniture, was painted the shade of dried mud. It didn't show dirt, Pap had boasted.

But my husband was undaunted. He labored on, up there near the ceiling, on his back, like Michelangelo. Stroke after stroke, night after night. Like falling hair, the bristles in our cheap brushes would get stuck in the wet paint or splat wayward brown globs on random surfaces. Frustration mingled with turpentine and oil-based paint and became the sweet smell of homeownership.

Days, a week or more, passed, but eventually the poo-colored undercoat dried, and the stain went on. After it dried, he finished the beams off with slick shellac. In time, the shellac dried too, but we learned that can take a season or two.

To my surprise and my husband's delight, the end result was remarkably close to a stained wood look. Pat and Dave came by and declared us extraordinary decorators. And, as they predicted, it was wonderful being their neighbors. It was a near-perfect time in our lives.

Decades later, when I revisited the house, I noticed that subsequent homeowners had not redone the beams. "Scaffolding" is a scary word, I guess. Leastwise, our paint job is still standing.

And so are we. Pat and Dave were transferred to another city, then, years later, would die in a plane crash. Divorce took a toll on other couples we knew back then. But we're still standing. Partly because of dumb luck. But partly, I think, because I had a husband willing to hunker up near the ceiling for weeks, brushing on poo-colored paint to make our home as perfect as he could. Because he had faith it would turn out to be a beautiful thing.

MY LIBRARY ROOM

MY HUSBAND WOULD SAY THAT WE BOUGHT our nothing-out-of-the-or-dinary suburban home because it has a walkout basement. That's an uncommon feature, we were surprised to learn, in our more-flat-than-not subdivision. The real reason, however, was its tiny front room.

"A library!" I said. I'd wanted a house with a library since I first read about them in English novels when I was a girl, since I'd first glimpsed them on TV in old black-and-white movies of the 1930s and '40s. In my imagination, people who had achieved "the good life" were always retiring to their home's "library" to talk or read or to be alone and ponder big decisions.

"Where?" my husband asked.

"Where?" the real estate agent asked.

"Why, here," I said, pointing to a little bitty room squished behind French doors that opened off the entry hall.

"Oh," my husband said.

"Oh," the real estate agent said.

I could tell that they were having trouble looking past the dark hunter green walls and the huge floral design on the draperies that did indeed shrink this little room to cell-like proportions.

"Are you sure this isn't the closet for the master bedroom?" my husband asked.

Seizing the moment, the agent jumped in. "It wouldn't be hard at all to knock out that wall next to the master and then turn this space into a closet to die for."

Why were they not impressed with the two walls lined with white enameled bookshelves that stretched from floor to ceiling? Didn't they see the deep, pretty crown molding that held the shelves in place? Why hadn't they noticed that the room had a large bay window that faced east toward the morning sun? And what about the hardwood floor and the fireplace with a mantel? "Look here and here and here and here," I said.

Why couldn't they imagine how this room would grow, with the walls painted in a calm, space-expanding ivory? Couldn't they see the light flooding in the bay window, once it was freed from the choking jungle flora of the draperies? And don't forget mirrors—we could add mirrors to reflect that light.

Couldn't they feel the warmth of the fireplace on a January day, themselves sinking deep into an easy chair beside the fire, their feet resting on an ottoman? And my boxes and boxes of books—my lifelong friends that would replace the doodads that now filled the shelves—surely they could appreciate the joy the books would bring into the room.

"Well, the house does have a big walkout basement," my husband said.

"Yes, it does," the agent said. "A great resell feature."

And so it was decided.

IN THE TWENTY-ONE YEARS THAT WE HAVE LIVED HERE, my husband has come to love our little library as much as I do. He might say it's the morning light that lures us there for breakfast coffee and the newspaper most every day. It's where we spot the first glimpse of spring in the trees along the street, where we luxuriate in summer's indolent display of flowers just beyond the window. And in winter, when all the world is pale and dim, the sun still rises in the east, lighting our mornings with promise.

Some—the grandchildren, for example—would say they like the room because it has those glass French doors that can be closed, shutting the grown-ups out. They like to sprawl across the wood floor to play board games or for long make-believe sessions with tiny figures and little cars. There's a small TV tucked into the shelves, too, and no one tells them to turn the volume down when they're in there with the doors closed.

Others, who come with problems to discuss, would say they like the privacy the doors afford when secrets must be whispered, answers sought. But it's also a good place for laughing conversation, a cozy retreat that pushes back at HGTV's "open concept" and soaring ceilings.

In the end, though, I think we all like the little library because it's filled with books, from floor to ceiling. Even those who don't much read books seem to understand that these spines contain every-thing we'll ever experience, from joy to despair, from the ignorance of people to their greatest insights. And from time to time, I pull a book off the shelves and hand it to one or another, to help them learn something they're seeking, or to amuse them, or to inspire them when I have no words to do so.

On the north side of the room, I tell them, they'll find the Kentucky voices—some of the best, if not the most famous, writers who've ever lived. There's Elizabeth Madox Roberts, Jesse Stuart, and James Still. Wendell Berry and Bobbie Ann Mason and youngsters like Silas House. Oh, and here's one by that nice woman I met at the bookfair last year.

To the west are the masters, Shakespeare, Faulkner, Steinbeck, Hemingway, and the Harvard Classics. Eudora Welty, Katherine Anne Porter. ...Up high are the anthologies, some I taught from, others I studied from. Down there are comfortable favorites, *Run with the Horsemen*, *Cold Sassy Tree*, *Watership Down*, all the Michener books. And over here, well, these are the ones I haven't gotten around to reading yet, and I make the joke that I can't die until all of them are read.

The books, like the old friends they are, remain constant in all seasons. Their presence and influence ground me, make me seem wiser than I am. On this January day, though, when the world's news bounces ever shriller off a gray, icy landscape, I am more interested in comfort than in wisdom.

"Come sit with me by the fire in the library, and let's read awhile," I say to my husband. "And close the French doors—let's shut the grown-ups out."

The Bit of Road That Lay
in My View

WHEN GOD SPEAKS

Grace strikes us when we are in great pain and restlessness....
Sometimes at that moment a wave of light breaks into our darkness,
and it is as though a voice were saying: "You are accepted."
—Paul Tillich, *The Shaking of the Foundations*

WHEN I TAUGHT SCHOOL BACK IN THE OLDEN DAYS—before emails, texts, or cheap inkjet printers—the principal kept us informed via the intercom. His powerful, bass voice would come booming out of the walls, disembodied, conveying in no uncertain terms all we needed to know to make it through the day. At the risk of being ridiculed by the irreligious and lectured by the pious, I admit I've often wished that God would speak to me via the intercom. I would have been less confused about what to do in a million different situations.

Oh, I'm clear on the Old Testament "Thou Shalt Nots" of the Ten Commandments. I navigate life by the New Testament's message of love, too, which pretty much boils down to "Love thy neighbor as thyself" (which I've observed is easier to give lip service to than to accomplish). But I am flawed and, like a child, I have selective hearing, deaf when I should be listening.

Thus, I've bumbled around more than necessary, especially when it came to things like not worrying about tomorrow. I've had difficulty being as carefree as the birds of the air and the lilies of the field. For this shortcoming, I blame the DNA passed down to me by my grandmother's Massachusetts Puritan ancestors. Plan and work—or starve to death—is hardwired into my personality.

Nevertheless, I've met the unforeseen challenges in my life without crumbling. One night, however, I almost did.

I LOOKED THE SAME AND LAUGHED AS OFTEN, but the accumulated stress of major life changes had left me with chronic tension in my muscles. Now, after a long weekend at our daughter's college graduation—the kind that's held outdoors under a hot, blazing sun and lasts for hours—I lay awake in bed with the worst headache I'd ever had. It was so bad that I considered the possibility I was having a stroke. The aspirin I'd taken, just in case I was, had not touched the throbbing pain.

My list of concerns that night was daunting, although I acknowledge that others—even I at other times in my life—have faced worse, faced more, without stumbling. The thing about crumbling, though, is that it doesn't always happen when it logically might be expected, even excused. It sneaks up on you, often in the dark, when you should be sleeping.

In the next few weeks, I had to prep and sell my dream house in a town I'd lived in for thirty years, the community where our children had been born and grown up, where I'd leave behind a lifetime of friends and memories. I also had to find a house to buy in another part of the state, where my husband was now working, pack up our possessions, and get us moved.

And the day after tomorrow, in a Hail Mary pass to save her vision, I had to fly with my mother to Florida for experimental eye surgery. Since we'd been warned that the operation would likely fail, I also had to figure out a way to take care of my fastidious and fiercely independent mother when she went stone blind. Her doctor estimated that would occur in about a month, maybe sooner, if the surgery were not successful.

Only a few years earlier, my father had been killed in an accident on their farm. When his tractor turned over on a slick January hillside, my world flipped, too. Mother, unable to drive, given her vision, felt she could not live alone in the country. She reluctantly left the land that five generations of our family had called home and moved to an apartment in Lexington. I was her only child, and my role in our relationship began to shift in silent ways we did not discuss as my mother coped with her compromised world of dislocation, declining health, and widowhood.

Then the epidemic of corporate convulsions afflicting many American companies in the 1990s began to rapidly change Ashland, Kentucky. Indeed, the small city we'd called home from the first week of our marriage was becoming Exhibit A in a documentary about the "Rust Belt." When we had arrived a lifetime earlier, the area had a dynamic, diverse economy and a vibrant community life. As a few smaller plants closed down for good and one after another of the larger industries laid off workers, the residents had continued to whistle in the dark, pretending all would be well.

But when the giant itself, Ashland Inc., my husband's employer, began to shudder, the region went into shock. Once listed among the fifty largest corporations in America by *Forbes* magazine, it began to contract. Over a period of a few years, Ashland Inc. would sell its largest operating division—the petroleum company, including the behemoth refinery at nearby Catlettsburg—move its corporate headquarters to a distant city, and sever all ties to the area that had given it birth generations earlier.

With the option of early retirement and full benefits, my husband was among the lucky. Yet my world felt as though it had been turned upside down again, as it had done when my father was killed and my mother moved from the farm. In time, I would come to understand that home is a place you never leave, that you carry pieces of it with you in your heart, in your memories, wherever you sleep. I also would come to love our new hometowns—Georgetown and later, Lexington. I would find the encouragement and support I needed in these college towns to begin to write, a dream that had lain dormant for decades. I would be happy.

But on this night, I was still grieving for the company that had shaped our lives and for the town that had nurtured us from early adulthood into middle age. Mostly, though, I was in a frantic state of worry about Mother.

Mother had been treated for early onset glaucoma for forty years. Her case had ever been fragile and less responsive to treatment than that of others. Now her glaucoma numbers had escalated to unprecedented levels, and her doctor had exhausted every medication. Within a matter of weeks, pressure this high would sever her optic nerves and she would be completely blind, he told us. Given the unique complications of her case, he could offer only one option to pursue. He urged her to consult with a world-famous doctor affiliated with the Bascom Palmer Eye Institute at Florida's University of Miami. She might be a candidate for an experimental surgery being performed there.

Getting Mother to Miami would be challenging. Extensive arthritis of the spine and complications from hip replacement surgery had dramatically limited her mobility. Furthermore, if she had surgery, she and I would need to remain in a Miami hotel for several weeks, we were told, for follow-up care. The pressing ordeal of getting our house ready to sell, buying another, and moving would be put on hold indefinitely.

Most of all, I was worried about how we would manage going forward if Mother were to lose her eyesight. She had fought this outcome relentlessly for decades. Now it seemed she'd lost the battle. Neither she nor I had a clue how one copes with complete blindness.

As I lay there with my head throbbing, listing all the life changes that loomed ahead of me in the next few weeks, my body began to tremble. Decades later, I now realize that I was in deep grief for what I can only vaguely describe as an accumulated sense of loss that had begun with my father's death. In that moment, however, I thought that I was indeed having a stroke. I was unable even to call out to my husband sleeping beside me.

That's when it happened. It wasn't a voice on the intercom. It wasn't a voice at all. It was more like the sensation of words, although that description eludes the experience I remember. "Your mother's eyesight will be okay."

There was no reason for me to think it would be okay. Her doctor adamantly thought it would *not* be okay. But suddenly, *I was okay.* A sense of peace—oh, something even more than peace—flowed through my body. I stopped trembling, my headache abruptly vanished, and I slept.

Two days later, I flew with Mother to Miami. With apprehension, we showed up early for her appointment with the famous doctor. In Lexington, her glaucoma pressure had been running forty-five to fifty-five for weeks. In Miami, it measured twelve and fourteen—on the low side of normal.

"Why are you here?" the famous doctor asked.

MOTHER DID NOT HAVE EYE SURGERY because she did not need it, the famous doctor said, and we flew back to Kentucky the next day. She would continue to have recurring challenges controlling her glaucoma in the years ahead, but she would retain functional vision until her death a decade later.

Some will say that is why I am telling this story, to give hope to others praying for medical miracles. And I do believe in hope, and I do pray for miracles.

But I've lived a long time, and I know that such prayers are not always answered. I have no explanation for why bad things happen to good people. I can only remind myself that the human body is mortal by definition and that like the writer of Corinthians, now I see through a glass, darkly.

I have been struck by grace, however, when I was restless and in great pain, have heard the wave of light break into my darkness, and reassured, I have slept, knowing that I am known, that I am not alone as I go on.

AN APRIL FOOL

I'M PARTIAL TO APRIL. Here in Kentucky, our redbud, crab apple, and pear trees wake up and go into a flowering frenzy, as though embarrassed by their winter nakedness. The racehorses run again at Keeneland. The songbirds return.

But the month does begin with April Fools' Day, the calendar's nod to practical jokers. It's my least favorite day of the year. I try to ignore it and push through to my birthday that comes around a week later. I blush even now, though, after a lifetime, when I remember the day that I was the biggest April Fool of all.

IN 1953, I WAS IN THE SECOND GRADE at New Columbus Grade School, where three teachers taught about seventy-five students in grades one through eight. With its coal-burning stove inside and the outhouse out back, it would have felt at home in the nineteenth century. Appearances can be deceiving, however.

Although we hung our coats in a "cloakroom," as our grandparents had done, and drank cistern water from a dipper, this was post-World War II America. Miss Louella Forsee, the county curriculum director over in Owenton, dropped in unexpectedly every few weeks to make sure we were on track for the state's annual achievement tests. And in Miz Zell True, we first and second graders had a down-home version of Maria Montessori (although I'm pretty sure Miz Zell never heard of her).

Now, here's the thing. I'd noticed that my beloved, laid-back teacher, Miz Zell, usually so confident and expansive, went to pieces when Miss Forsee arrived to observe our classroom. Like a surprise military inspection, her visits always caught us unawares. Someone near the window would happen to spot her gray Studebaker pull into the school's gravel lot. (The Studebaker looked oddly delicate and prissy compared to our parents' oversized, practical Fords and Chevys.) That someone would then sound the alarm: "Miss Forsee is here!"

The rest of us would join in. "Miss Forsee is here?" "Now?"

Then Miz Zell would fly into a predictable routine much like I do when unexpected guests phone that they're passing through town and are five minutes from my house.

Two more different women could not have entered the teaching profession. Miz Zell was tallish, and though she was not fat, she was on the sturdy side. Miss Forsee was petite and thin to the point of frailty.

Miz Zell spoke in a deep, resonant tone that might even be described as loud, and she favored washable, cotton wraparound dresses. Miss Forsee's voice was thin and high, like a bird's. She always dressed impeccably in a dark gabardine suit with a pastel blouse peeking around the lapels.

Miz Zell's hair was an unruly mass of snow-white fluff surrounding her face like a halo. Miss Forsee's dark permanent waves were held under tight control with numerous hairpins.

Miz Zell was nonchalant about schedules and tolerant of creative mess. She met each of her first and second grade students—poor and poorer, quick or slow or in between—where we were, and with prayer and theatrics, pulled us up and onward. She was probably the best teacher I've ever known.

Miss Forsee was about order and staying on the book. Her job was to help her teachers get their lagging-behind rural charges up to grade-level performance on the state's standardized achievement tests. I'm reminded that the angst over testing is not new—nothing in education is ever new, it only gets renamed. She, too, was a gifted, dedicated educator, and a huge heart rested in her tiny frame. I grew to love her over the years.

But on April 1, 1953, I was a full-of-myself, expressive kid, at the beginning of my lifelong love affair with the theater. I casually looked out the large window and, in my best surprised voice, said, "Miss Forsee is here!"

Immediately, the humorous panic I'd anticipated took over Miz Zell. She began to frantically straighten her desk, pat her hair, and apply lipstick. She ordered two of us to pick up any paper that might be on the floor and told the rest to "sit down, be quiet, and get to work."

The look I saw on that magnificent woman's face haunts me still. In that instant, I glimpsed the insecurity that can exist, even in adults, even an adult as capable as Miz Zell.

Years later, I would learn that she had not graduated from high school. In the early twentieth century, in rural places like Owen County, anyone who had completed the eighth grade successfully could take the county teacher's exam. If they passed, they could begin teaching without a high school diploma in a one-room school. Many exceptional students like Miz Zell took the exam when they turned sixteen. She'd taught in country schools for years on what was then called "a lifetime certificate," when she and I met up at New Columbus Grade School.

However, under Kentucky's new minimum foundation laws enacted in the early 1950s, her old county lifetime certificate was voided. She now was teaching on a probationary emergency certificate. It could be renewed each year if there were not enough certified teachers available to fill the classrooms, but renewal was not guaranteed. Despite her experience and skill, Miz Zell also earned a much lower salary than even a first-year teacher who had a college degree and full certification. At age fifty-nine, she was taking correspondence and summer college classes in a frantic effort to earn a late-in-life diploma. She would die less than three years later, still teaching, and one of the many things I regret about her early death is that she did not live to graduate.

In contrast, Miss Forsee, anchored in the county school superintendent's office, had multiple college degrees. As the county curriculum director, Miss Forsee's job was secure and important. Without intent to do so, her efficient, businesslike manner, paired with her fine education, intimidated Miz Zell and turned her into a puddle.

BUT I DIDN'T UNDERSTAND ALL OF THIS IN 1953. Not exactly. I only knew I'd glimpsed something in Miz Zell's face that a child did not want to see. I cried out, "April Fool!" to end my joke as quickly as I'd initiated it. There's no fun to be had at another's expense, I realized that day. I've never played an April Fools' prank on anyone again.

WHAT BOOKS HAVE MEANT TO ME

OUR YOUNGEST GRANDCHILD, GEORGIA JANE, is learning to read. She's in kindergarten at a shiny-new school filled with the most up-to-date everything. Seven hundred other students in grades K–5 learn with her. Like a traveler from a foreign country, I attempt to tell her about my first school, although she stares back at me with uncomprehending eyes. She cannot imagine such a strange place.

New Columbus had about seventy-five students in eight grades and only three teachers. Nothing was shiny about it, from the oiled pine floors to the coal-burning stoves that hunkered in the corner of each classroom. Nothing was up-to-date, even for 1951. We did not have a water fountain but plunged a dipper into a bucket of cistern water to fill our drinking cups. We went to the toilet in an outhouse out back. We didn't have a cafeteria but carried lunch boxes from home or ran across the road to Nick's Grocery for a cheese-and-bologna sandwich. We hung our jackets on hooks in an anteroom quaintly called a "cloakroom."

And yet we learned to read from books, just as Georgia Jane is doing. This, then, is what I would like for her to know about my lifelong journey with books. It is also my valentine to those special, talented individuals who teach reading, and to librarians, and to all educators who encourage students to keep on reading. Thank you. Thank you. Thank you.

MY FIRST TEACHER, MIZ ZELL TRUE, may have been a religious fanatic. I prefer to think of her as devout. What I remember is that she talked about miracles a lot, about Daniel in the Lion's Den, about Shadrach, Meshach, and Abednego, and that she taught me to read. I thought then—and still do now—that a love of books was the miracle Miz Zell asked God to grant me.

I knew on some primitive level that language distinguished us from the cows and sheep on our farm. Talking to each other was a large part of what it meant to be human. Even those I knew who were deaf, like our neighbor's little girl, or mentally impaired, like my mother's friend Elizabeth, sought ways to "talk." Now, as a reader, I had cracked the code of written language. And so I—a little Kentucky girl who lived at a crossroads called Natlee that you could barely find when you were standing right there, much less on a map—I could join a worldwide conversation. And I did.

Like the ancients around their prehistoric campfire, I began with stories. Mine were simple ones, like *The Bobbsey Twins* and *Nancy Drew* mysteries. In third grade, the bookmobile pulled into my world and lured me to the inspiring shelves of blue-bound biographies about America's great. I also read for information, about dinosaurs, about history in the *Little House on the Prairie* books, and about a gazillion other topics.

By seventh grade, felled by flu that lingered for weeks, I began to plow through my father's bookshelf of classics, *Robinson Crusoe*, *The Picture of Dorian Gray*, *Green Mansions*. Story made room for character and theme. My understanding of the world grew more complex.

In our small high school, English teachers like Joanne DeWitt and Eileen Morgan directed me toward the best of the best. (Am I the only one who hoards her school-days anthologies as though they were rare books?) In college, I declared as an English major the first week and never looked back. I was fortunate to enter higher education when classical surveys of English, American, and world literature were still mandatory. My professors plunged me into a vat of great writing and let me simmer.

I won't belabor my lifetime syllabus here because—and I'm not being disingenuous—I am embarrassed that it isn't longer. I haven't read enough. Still, as a reader, I've probably met every kind of person who ever was and have lived through most every human condition. I have stepped outside of myself, beyond my narrow place, and though I cannot see with the eye of God, I have caught a glimpse of all humanity.

As a young high school English teacher, I neglected diagraming sentences and spent most of my energy attempting to set my students on fire with my love for reading, a passion that I believed would nurture and sustain them long after they left my classroom. One day I stumbled upon an essay by Kentucky writer and teacher Jesse Stuart in which he, like me, was trying to explain to his students what books had meant to him. He concluded his beautiful elegy to literature with a powerful quotation from the early twentieth-century author Clarence Day Jr. I read Stuart's entire essay to my students, but when I came to

Day's words quoted at the end I began to cry. The teenagers thought, rightfully, that I was a little crazy because I do get crazy when I talk about the miracle of written language. But old Clarence had nailed in a few words what I had been fumbling to tell them.

Monuments fall, nations perish, civilizations grow old and die out, and after an era of darkness new races build others. But in the world of books are volumes that have seen this happen again and again, and yet live on, still young, still as fresh as the day they were written, still telling men's hearts of the hearts of men centuries dead.

Amen, Mr. Day. Amen.

ON MOTHERING

AFTER READING A PARENTING EXPERT'S COLUMN in the newspaper that makes it sound so easy, followed by receiving phone calls from my daughters who make it sound so hard, I realize, in retrospect, that I was a mess of a mother. I plucked tacky, plastic Halloween costumes off the rack at Kmart for my children. Fed them inorganic anything. Dressed them in environmentally destructive polyester because it didn't need ironing. Well, it's a miracle my kids didn't turn out to be sociopaths.

Take our first daughter. A screaming insomniac from the moment she came home from the hospital, she never went to sleep before midnight. I suppose she did once in a while out of exhaustion, but in my memory, she wandered around the house throughout the night from birth until she left for college. At about the age of two and a half, however, she was smart enough to stop screaming and learned to be quiet during her nocturnal revelry. Thus, I blissfully napped while she watched repeats of *Sesame Street* and *The Electric Company* on the family room TV.

She was the one who sent her kindergarten teacher into hand-wringing fits when she didn't draw stick people with a sufficient number of anatomical parts. The young teacher said this absence of detail reflected an alarming lack of reading readiness. Fearing that social services would descend upon me for having slept in the recliner while my toddler had watched Bert and Ernie and Cookie Monster, I didn't mention to the teacher that my daughter had learned to read fluently by the age of three watching PBS at midnight. However, I did worry that dehumanized stick people indicated that my kid was a potential sociopath.

I tried, then, to pump up her stick drawings. "Couldn't you add some squiggly hair, maybe in brown or yellow crayon, on top of your drawing?" I'd suggest. "Or maybe toss in some blue dots for eyes?" She stared at me like I was crazy. Then she explained, "I'm not a good draw-er," and went back to reading the morning newspaper.

Daughter Number One was also too quiet at school, which worried everybody to death, and her hair wouldn't cooperate either (which worried me to death). Later, no thanks to me, she would graduate from an Ivy League school, impress everyone she met with her reading readiness, and learn to make the best of her hair.

To our relief, Daughter Number Two slept like the books say babies are supposed to do. However, at about the age of eighteen months, she tossed the books out the window with a giggle and started to do things her way. If you put her in her room for a disciplinary time-out, she'd climb out the window and run to a neighbor's house to play. If you hid the cookies—or the knives or the scissors or your irreplaceable pearl earrings given to you on your wedding day—on the tip-top ledge of the cabinets in your two-story kitchen, she would scale the faux wood wall as if she were Sir Edmund Hillary conquering Mount Everest.

She could, however, draw fantastic stick people. This gave me hope during our darkest hours that she would not turn out to be, you know, a sociopath. Like the time she ordered her older sister to "turn the other cheek like Jesus says to do" so she could hit her again on the opposite side of her face. Like the time she skipped through Kroger chanting at the top of her lungs, "Johnny Jones poo-poos in his pants—" I walked really fast so people wouldn't know she was with me and managed to lose her in the produce department. I waited five minutes before claiming her when the store's loudspeaker shouted that they had a lost little girl in the office whose name was "Johnny Jones Poo-poos—"

Daughter Number Two was too talkative at school, which worried everybody to death. Her hair would not cooperate either (which worried me to death). Later, no thanks to me, she would graduate from college with honors, charm everyone she met with her effervescent personality, and learn to make the best of her hair.

Daughter Number Three picked up everything I didn't want her to do from both her older sisters, plus a moral objection to eating meat from that model of all things good and noble, Michael Jackson. I was too tired to care. I threw some dry cereal at her a few times a day, turned on PBS, and prayed she wouldn't grow up to be a sociopath. I did ask her middle sister—who turned out to be artistically gifted, despite blowing up her middle school pottery project in the kiln and flunking art for the semester—to teach her how to draw stick people, with or without anatomical parts.

Daughter Number Three was socially well adjusted in school, neither too quiet nor too talkative, which pleased everybody. Go figure. Grooving in benign neglect by then, I can't remember if her hair cooperated or not. Later, no thanks to me, she would earn a PhD in clinical psychology and learn to spot a sociopath from a distance of fifty yards.

I've never been asked to write a parenting column. That's probably because I don't have many answers, and I'm even a little shaky on what the questions are. But I am sure of this: new mothers should start teaching their babies how to draw stick people as soon as they get home from the hospital. The world does not need any more sociopaths.

MORSE CODE

I'M LEARNING MORSE CODE. I got the idea from a movie I saw this summer. In one of those light-bulb-flashing-over-my-head moments, I realized this could bridge the communication gap between my adult children and me. They only communicate by texting now, and with my clumsy old thumbs and last-century spelling, I'm left out of the conversation. Reinvent the telegraph, I say, with its finger-friendly dashes and dots in plain old English!

I've spent as long as forty-five minutes trying to type something on my itty-bitty iPhone screen that conveys, *Yes, I can meet you in fifteen minutes for lunch. Say where?* When my thumbs finally end up with *yex whrrz?* they text back, *LOL we missed u at lun TTYL*. They're sweet like that, always sending me *lots of love*, even though I can't text worth a cent. I'm sorry I missed going to that new restaurant, TTYL, though.

Why didn't you just call them, I hear you asking. ROTFL!!! I DID, but they no longer answer their cell phones. Their ringers are turned off, because OMG!!! talking on the phone is so last century, and RBTL (one has to have boundaries in the contemporary world—not be tied to a ringing phone, even if your BFF is calling, much less your DP). BTW, they don't have landlines either because in their POV only a spendthrift would waste money on that.

This is not the first time in my life I've been disconnected. I spent my childhood in a world without telephones because the corporate magnates thought it unprofitable to build lines across the hilly, rural areas of Kentucky. People don't believe me when I dredge up these details from my past—"TMI," my girls might say—and I agree that my childhood does sound like something out of *Little House on the Prairie*. At times, I have trouble believing me, too.

We lived within fifty to sixty miles of Cincinnati, Lexington, and Louisville, in the center of what politicians now call Kentucky's Golden Triangle, but there were only three telephones in the community. Back in the 1920s, a cooperative had raised money to build a phone line, and those who bought in were allowed to join the secret society of phoners. If you missed out at the beginning, you were forever shut out. People actually bequeathed their plug-in to the party line in their wills. The closest phone to us was at the Natlee store, and I don't recall anyone in our family ever using it except to call the doctor or an ambulance.

We did have postcards, which, now that I think about it, were an early version of texting. For a penny, later two, you could drop a few lines in the mail and the recipient would get them—I know you're not going to believe this—the very next day! Aunt Bessie would send a message on Thursday that she'd like to come over for dinner on Sunday. Mother would write back, *Great, see you then.* It was an efficient system if one's handwriting were legible, which Aunt Bessie's was not.

Ma Bell finally relented sometime during the late 1950s and brought telephone service into the countryside for all who wanted it. Overnight, a big black dial-up phone wired us into the twentieth century. In an arrangement that discouraged young love, ours sat on a table at the end of the living room sofa, next to the television. When a boy rang me up, Daddy refused to relinquish his nearby easy chair or turn down the TV, even if the poor fellow was calling long distance from a pay phone and dropping quarters in every couple of minutes.

Privacy didn't matter anyway, I guess, since we were on an eight-family party line. Out of curiosity or boredom, unidentified others were always picking up their receivers somewhere along the road to eavesdrop on our stuttering conversations. Some, impatient to use their phones, simply clicked their receivers up and down to hurry us along.

As time went on, we added something called "extensions." That meant we could have a phone in the kitchen and in the bedroom, as well as in the living room. Extension phones, especially in a color other than black, became a status symbol. In our first place, I went with beige receivers because in those days I was on the cutting edge of home décor.

Cordless phones were the next big breakthrough. This meant I could talk on a phone anywhere in the house. We bought a six-phone packaged set, and I knew I had achieved the American Dream. Our three daughters loved talking on the phone back then. Of course, everyone they wanted to talk to was a long-distance tariff call away. I spent hours sorting through complicated long-distance plans trying to get the most minutes for the dime.

But all that was before texting. Now I am reduced to communicating with the family on one tiny phone that stays in my purse near the back door so I don't forget it when I go out. It can't be heard anywhere else in the house, should it ring, which of course, it doesn't, since text messages only go *bonk*, once, briefly. Some nights, after I've been writing upstairs at my computer all day, I'll find a whole string of text acronyms from the girls, and finally an all caps scream of despair, *W R U*? Well, I want to say, I'm right here by my beige, cordless, landline phone at my computer which, BTW, receives email.

This is why I'm learning Morse code. IMO everything old is new again, so I'm going back to the nineteenth century and will show them what classy texting looks like! THX for listening and B4N. XOXO & LYLAS, Georgia.

NAMES

IT WAS A JOYFUL MORNING AT THE MAKE-BELIEVE CIRCUS. The children sang big top songs as loud as they could, and on cue, they cackled like monkeys and roared like lions. The two-year-old class at our grandson's nursery school was in rare form for the end-of-the-year program.

Sadly, though, Charles and Donnie missed the show. Roger, Richard, and Jerry weren't there either, and neither was Ed.

To be honest, they would have felt out of place. All the other little boys had first names that could be confused for last names (Parker, Conner, or Blake) or that end with an *N* and vaguely rhyme (Aidan, Brayden, and Jayden). Although it doesn't rhyme with much of anything, I realized how lucky we were to have a spare surname lying around in our family that also concludes with the letter *N*. Maybe our Hudson has both trends covered? Frankly, he can use the edge. Given the challenges he's faced with potty training, he probably could not have survived the nursery school playground with a quaint moniker like Clarence.

Although I think the names currently in vogue for little boys—and little girls, too—are charming and beautiful, I miss my old playmates. Nobody told me they'd followed Myrtle the Dodo Bird into extinction.

A quick search of the Social Security website confirmed my worst fears. The popular girls of my youth—Barbara, Linda, Sharon, Pat, Judy, Carol—are now wallflowers. They sit on the sidelines at the baby-naming cotillion with unfilled dance cards, watching Olivia, Madison, Isabella, and Mia fend off legions of admirers. And the cute boys I pined for—the cool Garys, the trendy Ronnies, the athletic Larrys—are about as out of the loop as the Elmers, Chesters, and Adolphs.

And so I think it's time I organize a support group for people whose names went out with the Eisenhower administration. I have experience, after all, at being in with the out crowd. My Georgia peaked in popularity in 1894, with a rank of eighty-five, and has been going downhill ever since, according to the Social Security folks who keep track of these things. It hung on by its fingernails to position 305 in the most recent list. The male equivalent, George, hasn't fared much better, despite the political clout of presidents one, forty-one, and forty-three (plus cinema heartthrob George Clooney.)

Members of Over-the-Hill-Names-Anonymous (OTHNA) might commission research to better understand why a particular name suddenly falls off the hit parade. Understanding this could help one take the snubs less personally. However, after reviewing the extraordinary data the Social Security website provides, I've concluded it's the same reason that makes anything else go out of fashion—if your parents owned it, liked it, or wore it, it's verboten.

For example, Linda, the number one name for girls in the years 1947–1952 and who lingered in the top ten until 1965, came in at 825 last year. Obviously, Linda is your grandmother or her sister. She probably has gray hair, albeit with frosted blonde tips, and wears comfortable shoes with good arch supports. She definitely wouldn't fit in at nursery school.

But what causes a name to become trendy in the first place at a particular moment in time? Olivia and Sophia, consistently among the top five most popular names for baby girls born in the last fifteen years, didn't get a mention in the top few hundred the year I was born. That gives them the advantage of distance from the Medicare generation, but I didn't go to school with anyone named Bertha either, so why, then, Sophia or Olivia? I would give Sophia Loren and Olivia de Havilland the credit—movie and TV stars often inspire naming trends—but I doubt anyone having a baby last year knows who they are. No, I think it's something more profound. I think it's the zeitgeist.

The "zeitgeist," according to the dictionary, means the "spirit of the times." It's the mood of an era, the intellectual and cultural climate of a nation. What it really means is that five people get together in the school bathroom in fifth grade, while you're on the playground eating a baloney sandwich, and make all the important decisions for your generation. Then they come out and hypnotize you and make it all seem like it's your idea to start with.

Take me. I named our first child Shannan because I liked the sound of its soft assonance, and paired with Stamper, it had the benefit of alliteration, too. Mostly, though, I chose it for uniqueness. I'd known only one other Shannan, male or female, in my entire life. So—yes, you guessed it—that name, variously spelled, leaped from nowhere into the top twenty names for girls the year she was born. Like a disco dancer, it made a great, big splash in the 1970s and then glided out of the spotlight.

Stung by my failed attempt at originality, I opted to use an old-fashioned family name when our second daughter was born. Nobody else likes those kinds of names, right? My stillborn sister had been named Rebecca after my father's grandmother, and so Shannan's sister would be named for mine. That very year, Rebecca catapulted to the tenth most popular name for girls, although it had loitered in the low one hundreds for most of the twentieth century. In fact, the year our Becky was born, and the next, marked the zenith of the name's popularity in all of history. It began to decline in the late 1970s, and last year, it slid in at 148.

When our third daughter came along, I decided to beat this name biz at its own game. I christened her Georgia in giddy anticipation of riding her coattails to a popularity our name had never known. Alas, the zeitgeist refuses to be manipulated.

So, members of OTHNA, we must strive to remember that "over the hill" is only a synonym for "waiting for another turn." By the way, have I told you about my Great-Uncle Ethelbert Hudson and his brother Ditzler and their sister Gertrude? Now, those are names waiting for their zeitgeist to come in.

QUEEN ELIZABETH AND ME

MY ANCESTRY.COM DNA TEST RESULTS CAME BACK, and it turns out I have a shot at challenging Queen Elizabeth's claim to the throne. I have more British genes than she does. This doesn't surprise me. Her people kept fooling around with European royalty, while my folks married up with whoever lived on the nearest farm. Proximity continued to be the driving force in my family's mating rituals, even after we moved over to America three hundred years ago. We are a pragmatic tribe.

I had hoped my DNA might reveal intriguing mysteries about my prehistory. A little Genghis Khan would have been titillating. After all, he is said to have more descendants than any other man who ever lived. Apparently, however, I am not one of them, which may explain my aversion to conflict and aggression.

A smidge of the Iberian Peninsula would have been exotic, but since I sunburn if I walk outside before six in the evening, Portuguese, Spanish, or Moroccan DNA pulsing through my genes was too much to hope for. The same goes for the coast of West Africa. I am left to make do with a faint hint of Sweden and a sniff of "Germanic Europe"—hardly the stuff of a juicy novel.

But back to Queen Elizabeth II. For a long stretch of my childhood and early teens—long before I'd heard about DNA—I prepared myself to take over her job someday. That can't be coincidence. Destiny, I believe, was nudging me to right the wrongness of history.

My plan to ascend to the English throne was straightforward, not devious. I'd *marry* into the royal family. I'd seen pictures of her son Prince Charles in *LIFE Magazine*, and he looked cute and pleasant. I also liked his house. It had good bones, and I figured I could do a lot with it. Brighten it up, *Better Homes & Gardens* style, you know? And I read that it came with a cook, too.

So I started walking around with a book on my head to improve my posture, read a lot of English novels, practiced smiling, and began carrying a purse everywhere I went. The snag in my plan to snag a marriage with Prince Charles was that old proximity issue. He never visited Owen County, Kentucky, and I couldn't even get my picture in *LIFE Magazine*, much less get to London.

Though my youthful reach for the crown exceeded my grasp, my efforts had their own rewards. In particular, I learned that I have an inborn knack for carrying a purse on my arm. I don't hold it when I'm taking a bath, as I suspect Queen Elizabeth may do, but I have it nearby even then. I take it everywhere—on a hike, on a carousel ride, everywhere. I don't mean to sound snobby, but when you're a genetic near miss to the English throne, it's what you're born to do.

I rely on a purse to keep essentials at my fingertips. It holds money, credit cards, and my photo ID; a comb and cosmetics; a can of Diet Coke, in case I get thirsty; a candy bar, if my glucose crashes;

my phone; and a magazine, if I get bored. Oh, and glasses. Sunglasses, two pairs—a good one and a cheap one—and two pairs of reading glasses, in case one breaks. When my children were babies, my purse did double duty as a diaper bag, too.

Still, I wonder what the Queen carries in her purse? Surely she doesn't need a photo ID since her image is pictured on her country's money. Indeed, I've heard that the Queen never handles money at all, leaving the distasteful task of paying for whatever she wants to others, to preserve the illusion of, well, I'm not sure what the illusion is, but apparently, money is not to be spoken of. And when she needs the other things that I consider purse essentials, an assistant would quickly provide them to her.

I've decided she carries Kleenex in her purse. What else would she need on the spur of the moment, while shaking hands at a Garden Club luncheon, that an aide would not promptly provide her? But if you needed a Kleenex in a hurry, how could you discreetly ask someone to get it for you before the need was obvious? Yes, it has to be Kleenex and nothing else at all. Otherwise, at the age of ninety-umpteen, she'd need a shoulder replacement by now from carrying around a too-heavy purse.

Personally, I think that Elizabeth would have been happier with me as a daughter-in-law than with—those others. If you can believe a reliable source like the *National Enquirer*, she wasn't too thrilled about either of them. She and I could have filled our family visits discussing the pros and cons of a good pocketbook, and she would love that I love the horse farms of Kentucky. But Charles has turned out to be rather dull, and honestly, I think his mother will outlive him.

In the meantime, I've lived happily ever after with my homegrown prince. And in retrospect, I realize that my ancestors *did* retake the throne for our family when they emigrated to America. Here, everyman is his own king and everywoman her own queen.

SIRI

I FIRED MY PERSONAL ASSISTANT. I got worried she was a spy for the CIA, using my ho-hum life as a front. Bumbling around working for me, a Kentucky grandmother on Medicare, she was respectably dull and invisible, ready to take on any ISIS terrorists who may have penetrated the frozen foods section of my local Kroger. If not an undercover agent, however, she certainly was the most incompetent assistant in history. Or maybe the most impertinent.

I hired Siri a few years ago when she hailed me at the Apple Store. She was mysterious, lingering somewhere just out of sight behind a brightly lit display, and to this day, I couldn't tell you what she looks like. But that voice—I couldn't identify her accent, but it lured me in. It was vaguely foreign, but obviously she had learned to speak English at someplace impressive, maybe Oxford.

"What can I do to help you?" she asked, all high-toney sounding. Before she asked, I hadn't known I needed any help, but now that she had, I realized that maybe I did.

"Well," I said, "I guess I could use someone to assist me with this and that when I'm out driving."

"Like what?" she asked.

I'm not usually open with strangers about my shortcomings, but her helpful tone encouraged me to answer with candor.

"I don't always know how to get to where I need to go." There. I'd admitted it. "If I had someone to call who would look up directions and verify addresses, I wouldn't get lost as often as I do."

Without hesitation, Siri said, "I can do that for you."

"And if I had someone who would ring up my friends or family members on my iPhone while I'm driving, I'd be a safer driver." I hated admitting that, too, but it was true.

Siri said, "Yes, I can place calls for you."

"Could you also take dictation and send a typed text message or an email on my behalf?" I was warming to the idea of an on-call helper.

"Yes!" she said.

"And what if I needed to locate a bedbug-free hotel in a strange city?"

"I could research that information for you on the internet in seconds," she answered.

And so our relationship began. From the outset, however, it was apparent that we were not destined to be BFFs. For starters, Siri had no sense of humor. The first day she was on the job, my granddaughter Eliza—with her adolescent grasp of comedy—asked her to solve a funny little riddle. Without sarcasm, Siri responded, "I do not comprehend. These are some of the things you may ask me." And then she began a recitation of topics unrelated to my granddaughter's question.

Perhaps I should qualify—Siri has no sense of humor unless the joke is on me. For example, this same granddaughter told her I preferred to be called "Swag Money." Obviously, this is not an appropriate name to call your employer, and Siri, with all her education, knows this. Yet, to this day, despite my many reminders to address me as Georgia, Siri begins every conversation with "Swag Money..."

Which brings me to my Kentucky accent. Last week, I asked her to call Patsy for me. Patsy is one of my best friends and I call her often, but so there would be no confusion, I said slowly and with perfect enunciation, "Call PATSY."

"Swag Money, you want to call SEXY? I am sorry, but you have no SEXY on record," Siri said without even a giggle.

"Not SEXY. PATSY. Call PATSY."

"Calling PAT'S STEAKHOUSE," Siri answered.

Or maybe I'd ask her to call Ernie, my husband.

"Swag Money, you want to call IRELAND?" Siri would respond. "What city in Ireland?"

"Not Ireland. Call ERNIE."

"Swag Money, I am sor-ry. I cannot locate the city of Ernie in North Ireland. Is there anything else I can help you with?"

"YES. CALL ERNIE STAMPER. And I'm GEORGIA, not Swag Money!"

"Swag Money, there is no Bernie Camper in Ima, Georgia, listed in your contacts. May I call someone else for you?"

"YES! ERNIE! And this is GEORGIA, not Swag Money!"

"Swag Money, I cannot comprehend. You have no contact for Ernie Georgia."

Then to add insult to injury, Siri would say in a patronizing tone, "Swag Money, THESE are some of the things I can help you with..."

"As if she would," I'd mutter under my breath.

Still, I held out hope that Siri would learn on the job, and I'd give her another chance. Maybe I'd ask her to double-check an address, let's say on Ireland Street in Lexington, Kentucky. Siri would say, "Swag Money, I am sor-ry. I cannot locate an Ernie Street in Lexington, Lucky."

"NOT ERNIE STREET, IRELAND STREET! KENTUCKY! NOT LUCKY!"

"Swag Money, do you want directions to Bernie Street in Ireland or Bernie Street in Lucky, Kentucky?"

"Never mind," I said. "Swag Money will get lost all by herself."

When it came to locating bedbug-free hotels, Siri admitted she was not up to that part of her job description. "Swag Money, I do not comprehend," she would say as she hung up on me.

And forget dictating texts or emails for her to type and send. Sheez—between Siri's hateful attitude and autocorrect, it's a wonder I didn't end up getting arrested for threatening the president or somebody. That would have amused Siri's perverse personality—to use me as a front, if she were a secret agent, *and* to get me in trouble with the government at the same time.

Then again, she could be an alien from outer space. She has been oddly secretive about her background, if you ask me, with that murky accent and feigned ignorance.

But what do I care? I've given her a pink slip. She's somebody else's problem now.

THE BREEDERS' CUP

THE BREEDERS' CUP GALLOPS INTO LEXINGTON next weekend. Since it's about the biggest do in horse racing, our town is putting on its company best. From abundant flowers to stunning street murals and gourmet food trucks, we're looking good. We've even gilded the lily and made Keeneland—already one of the prettiest places in America—lovelier and more accommodating.

Although I celebrate Lexington's opportunity to host this world-class event, I don't plan to attend. The reasons why I won't go? Well, you knew a story was coming, didn't you?

First of all, a girl from Natlee should have more common sense than to sit outside at a racetrack in Kentucky in tobacco-stripping weather. Second, a famous horse-racing event should not be held in Kentucky during tobacco-stripping weather (see first point, above). It should occur on the first Saturday of May, when tulips are blooming and all is well in the Commonwealth.

In 1988, however, I was persuaded to attend the first Breeders'

Cup ever held in Kentucky. Louisville's fabled Churchill Downs hosted the event, having snatched it away from the likes of California's Hollywood Park and Santa Anita. At the time, it was generally conceded that the "horse people" had agreed to shiver in a Louisville November out of respect for Kentucky thoroughbred owner and breeder John R. Gaines. Gaines had conceived the idea of the Breeders' Cup in 1982 as a way to improve racing's image.

"Persuaded" is an imprecise verb that covers a lot of territory. In my case, it included the opportunity to purchase a new outfit and spend two nights away from full-time motherhood. My husband's employer, Ashland Inc., had assigned him to host an official who represented a Middle Eastern oil company. This foreign company was a major supplier of crude oil at a time when the United States relied heavily on imported petroleum to function and often faced fuel shortages. Moreover, these Middle Eastern suppliers had to be cajoled into selling their crude oil (at sky-high prices) to American companies instead of selling it to, oh, say, Russia. And so, when the official—who owned a racehorse himself—had hinted in various conversations that he would like to be entertained at the Breeders' Cup, arrangements were made to do that. By the way, he said, his wife wanted to come, too.

Charged with keeping America's gas tanks full and the world safe for democracy, I went forth to do my civic duty and bought one of the most beautiful suits I've ever owned. It was a cream-colored wool crepe with little seed pearls festooning wide lapels, and fearing it might be cool on November 5, I selected a matching wool cape to layer over the suit, if needed. Delicate cream-on-cream embroidery spilled down the cape's front—but I digress. This was not about me but about America's security, as I explained to my husband when he saw the credit card bill.

On November 5, we woke to rain in Louisville, and in my memory, it did not let up until after night had fallen. The temperature never reached higher than fifty degrees. It hovered lower much of the day.

I started out with optimism, however. I had an umbrella, after all, and my wool cape, though thin, to add warmth to my suit. And, of course, we could always remain inside the clubhouse if the weather were too unpleasant.

The other wife, assigned to me to entertain, emerged in a full-length mink coat that brushed the top of her feet. A matching fur hat covered her ears. She was not a small woman, and, God forgive me, she looked exactly like Russia's one-time leader Khrushchev. She went on to say how much she loved horse racing and how thrilled she was to attend the Breeders' Cup, the thoroughbreds' "World Series." "I don't want to miss a single minute of this magnificent event," she said. And she didn't.

In 1988, Churchill Downs had not yet undergone the extensive renovations that would later turn it into a country club on steroids. We had box seats in what was then considered a prime location, but they were *outside*. Cover, however, was provided a short distance behind us in a comfortable, glassed-in clubhouse. Alas, Mrs. Khrushchev would not go inside. Not once. The husbands abandoned us for a dry roof early on, but we remained seated outside in the drizzling rain. "I can't bear to miss a moment of this excitement!" she kept saying as I kept smiling and smiling and smiling.

Huddled under my umbrella with my "respectable cloth" cape tucked around me, my wet feet cold and numb, I confess to breaking the tenth commandment. I coveted Mrs. Khrushchev's mink coat! Forget PETA—a mink coat might keep me from slipping into hypothermia and dying in front of seventy-one thousand people. What would a spectacle like that do to America's supply of crude oil, I wondered?

I survived the afternoon by discreetly confiding to Mrs. K that I had a "medical problem" that required me to step inside briefly to the ladies' room once every hour. "Can I bring you back some hot coffee?" I'd ask each time I left our box. "Oh, no. I'm fine, thank you," Mrs. K would reply, lifting her binoculars with a gloved hand to clarify a slight movement on the far side of the track.

The legendary Alysheba won the biggest race that day, the Breeders' Cup Classic. But the 1988 Breeders' Cup may best be remembered for the Distaff, a race for fillies. Personal Ensign, appearing hopelessly beaten at the top of the stretch, persevered and won by a head over Derby champion Winning Colors. I didn't fold either. I smiled through chattering teeth until the end of the seventh race on one of the most miserable days in Kentucky racing memory—and I'm proud to say that America did not run out of crude oil that winter. We girls from Natlee close strong.

ANOTHER BIRTHDAY

I GOT CAUGHT IN THE TAILWIND of my old friend Birthday, as he raced through another April. I admit that I lost my balance for an hour or two. "You're old," Birthday taunted as he flew past me on his way to outrun next year before I could blink.

"That's not nice," I shouted after him. "And besides, Old is the new New. Old, now that the baby boomers are on Medicare, is *in*."

I was bluffing, of course. Old has never been *in*. But it did occur to me that I have reached an age where I've learned a few things that might be helpful to others.

For example, I could tell aspiring English majors that it's okay if they don't find Shakespeare's comedies funny. His tragedies are unsurpassed, and his love sonnets are among the most beautiful in the English language, but Will would have been fired from most any sitcom writing staff, in my opinion. There. I've said it. I've committed literary heresy. If, however, you find yourself in a situation where you must sit through one of his comedies, it is politic to laugh. Guffaw *and pretend* that you believe the boy believes the girl is a boy, and the girl believes that the boy is a girl, and the other girl believes they're both boys, and they believe she is a boy. Otherwise, people will think you are too dumb to be an English major.

That's another advantage of being older. You realize that you're not as dumb as you thought you were. I don't know about you, but I've spent most of my adult life wandering through a forest of very tall trees without a map—not exactly lost, but unsure of my way through. I assumed other people had the map. Now I'm not so sure they did. I think they may often have felt dumb, too. Regardless, the route I've wandered has worked out well enough for me, even if it was not the same as others took.

But I'm also not as smart as I once thought I was either, and I apologize to those who had to put up with me in my arrogant youth when I assumed all knowledge (any worth having, at least) was within my grasp. And I'm certainly not as smart as many of my Facebook friends who have confident answers for all the world's problems. Every day, I learn something I didn't know about something else. I realize now that the earth and the people who inhabit it are more complex than I had dared imagine.

I *have* learned that drugstore skin products are as good as the expensive department store brands, if you don't object to cheap containers that break. And it's easier to be kind to everybody than it is to be selectively nice only to people you think might further your own interests.

You'll be happier if you surround yourself with flowers—or whatever you find beautiful. And contrary to bumper sticker philosophy, at the end of life, I suspect most of us *will* wish we had spent just a little more time cleaning out our closets.

It sounds trite to say, "Be grateful for what you have," but trite gets that way because it's grounded in truth. Our "haves" will differ from another's—and even within our own lives as time passes. This spring, I'm thankful to have my husband restored to good health after a life-threatening illness this winter.

Get as much formal education as is within your grasp. A flabby mind is no more attractive than a flabby body. I know a few notable exceptions, but it's easier to do this when you're young, before you marry or begin a family. On the other hand, it's never too late to begin.

Life will be easier if you can find something to work at that people will pay you to do. And while I believe in dreaming big, few of us are really cut out to be international diplomats, despite the proliferation of college degrees in that field.

Let me encourage you to give religion a chance—or at least a break. Nonbelief is all the rage now—though proselytizing, organized atheists seem an oxymoron to me. I admit that these sex scandals and random bigoted rants have shaken me, not to mention the un-Jesus-like plunge into politics some ministers have taken. But in my experience, it's usually church folk who show up to help wherever trouble strikes. This I know—faith has pulled my heart to a more loving, more generous and forgiving place.

Finally, I think that most of us end up accomplishing in life whatever is most important to us—whether we understand that is what we are doing or not. For me, I realize, that has been creating a family. As an only child, I grew up in a loving home but always longed for a bigger crowd around the table. Ours overflows now with six grandchildren, our three daughters, and our sons-in-law. They're not a perfect crew, but they're about as good as you'll run across.

So mock me if you will, Birthday boy. As soon as I dust myself off, I'll catch up with you. It'll be fun racing with you to next year. You may be surprised, though, at all I have planned. It may not even be too late for me to run for president.

HONEY

You see, of course, if you're not a dunce,
How it went to pieces all at once,—
All at once, and nothing first,—
Just as bubbles do when they burst.
> —Oliver Wendell Holmes, "The Deacon's Masterpiece or,
> the Wonderful 'One-hoss Shay'"

THE SIXTIES ARE THE NEW FORTIES, they said, the seventies the new fifties, and I believed them. I was striding through late middle age without a stumble when I bumped smack into Honey.

"Honey, can I do anything else for you today?" the young clerk at the cosmetic counter said. Her words, shaped in shining, ghost-like lip gloss, slapped me across the cheek like a cold wind on Heathcliff's moors.

Granted, my neck and jawline have let me down lately, but would she have called Meryl Streep "Honey?"

It happened again in the fast-food drive-through line. "That'll be six ninety-eight. Pull up to the next window, Honey."

Yes, I had asked one of the mumble-jumble generation to repeat the amount. As my father often pointed out, kids today aren't taught to enunciate. I gave her my Meryl-Streep-playing-Margaret-Thatcher-in-her-prime stare as I handed her a five and two ones and waited for my two cents worth of change.

Then I started bumping into Honey every which way I turned. I upped my Meryl Streep impersonation of Thatcher in hopes of an Oscar nomination. To amuse my nail technician, I threw in a little Queen of Cambodia, too, since he once had said I looked like her. That helped until my hair started falling out.

"Male-pattern baldness," the dermatologist said. "Nothing much can be done."

Numbers that matter to doctors crept upward. My sciatic nerve went out without me. My feet slid into flats and refused to leave. Still, I was sailing through middle age pretty well, I thought.

Then, like the Deacon's wonderful one-hoss shay (to paraphrase Oliver Wendell Holmes) that was built in such a logical way and then, of a sudden, it—ah, but stay. I'll tell you what happened last week without delay.

It began on a Friday as I walked into the Baptist church where my Aunt Georgia's funeral was shortly to commence. "Let's dart into the women's room," I said to my cousin. We'd been on the road for an hour and a half, and I was planning ahead for a confinement of unknown duration.

The restroom we located at the end of a long hallway was small and dark, but it provided a tiny, narrow cubicle. Indeed, I've rarely seen a public cubicle that narrow, and I quickly decided that backing in was the most prudent approach. It was not. Too late—oh, too late—I realized that the top on the commode was down.

My cousin urged me not to worry, that the scent of the funeral flowers would conceal all missteps. I was not convinced. The only thing to do, I decided, was to rinse my washable-Chico's-knit pants in the bathroom's itty-bitty sink. Channeling Meryl Streep, the Queen of Cambodia, *and* Margaret Thatcher, I stood tastefully dressed in pearls, blouse, suit jacket, and underwear and swished the legs of my pants in a minute basin of water.

If anyone had walked in, I was prepared to say this was a sanctioned form of baptism in the *Methodist Book of Discipline*. (Baptists think Methodists are heathen anyway.) Then, there being no hand dryer but only paper towels, I pulled on my wet, clean slacks and entered the sanctuary for the funeral.

That was on Friday. On Monday night, I completely mangled our hostess's freshly landscaped flower bed when backing my car out of her driveway in the dark after book club meeting. Tuesday, my three-year-old granddaughter spotted ninety-plus-year-old Betty White on television and started shouting, "Grandmommy, Grandmommy!" By Wednesday, I was burning boiled eggs.

"How do you burn boiled eggs?" my husband asked.

"Don't ask," I replied. I didn't mention that I'd also left an empty oven on for two hours.

On Thursday, I went to the ophthalmologist for my annual eye exam. I knew I was in trouble when he stopped smiling and started asking questions. "Do you smoke? Do you have high blood pressure? Did you notice your vision getting blurry?" No, no, and no, I answered. "Well, you've had an occlusion in the central vein in your right eye," he said. I managed to ask, "You mean I've had a stroke?" No, no, he reassured me. "It's only called a 'stroke' if it happens in your brain. If it happens in your heart, we call it a heart attack. This, well, this is an ocular occlusion, like I said."

"What causes that?"

"Well, several things. Sometimes a brain tumor, sometimes—" I stopped listening after "brain tumor."

I AM NOW IN THE SECOND WEEK OF MY DOTAGE. I'm happy to report that I do not have a brain tumor. Whew. I realize that I don't like boiled eggs all that much anyway—or, for that matter, cooking. Fortunately, as I pointed out to my husband, we live near a plethora of restaurants. I also have a greater appreciation of funeral flowers. They smell good no matter what.

Oliver Wendell Holmes did not say this—though he may have, because he was a very smart man who had the misfortune to live before Facebook—but take it from me, getting old is not for sissies, Honey.

Average Angels

THE CLASS OF 1963

TWELVE OF US, THE "GIRLS OF SUMMER," I quipped, met to eat Willie Whoppers on a hot August day at The Smith House, the same little place where we discovered them when we were teenagers. We assured each other that we were near unchanged, but even our old-fashioned names—two Judys, Sherry, Hattie, Fannie, Lucy, Mary, Sondra, Sally, Jean, Rita, Georgia—exposed the years that had passed since we left high school a half century ago.

Ours was the last small class to move through the nation's school system, and no one paid much attention to us. No one had to hire an extra teacher for us or build a larger building. Born in the final months of World War II, we were supposedly exempt from any childhood anxieties related to being a kid during the war. And in truth, we *were* a docile group, demanding little, unlike the noisy boomers who came nipping at our heels. We did as we were expected to do, even if that meant balancing our adult lives on the dizzy high wire that divided June Cleaver's world from Gloria Steinem's.

We graduated from high school in the spring of 1963, perhaps the American girl's last moment of moonlight and roses. I owned a wardrobe of madras plaid and dyed-to-match cashmere sweater sets. John F. Kennedy was living in the White House, and his wife, Jackie, was my role model in all things, down to the pillbox hat I wore to church on Sunday mornings. When I entered college that fall, I was required to wear a dress and high heels at dinner in the dining hall each evening. We had a nightly curfew, too—woe unto the wayward girl who wasn't inside the dorm when the doors were locked.

We all know how 1963 ended. My classmates and I lost our collective virginity when a rifleman raped us of our innocence in Dallas, Texas. The pill soon made curfews and locked dormitories superfluous. Pantsuits and denim replaced cashmere. Fast food overran slow food. Two-lane highways gave way to interstate freeways. Encyclopedias turned into computers that morphed into tiny phones slipped into our purses. Polio was eradicated. AIDS became a household word.

If we were able to master the acrobat's balancing act between Cleaver and Steinem, we still could not avoid the free fall that dropped us into the front seat of history's roller coaster. From Elvis to rap. From Civil Rights marches to a Black president. From Vietnam to Afghanistan. We rode the big ride, the one that takes the curves fast, but we hung on and survived to tell the tale.

WE GIRLS OF SUMMER LAUGHED as we resurrected old anecdotes, even as we quietly tallied those classmates who were no longer with us. We traded small talk about the weather and traffic and current events.

Then, after the pie plates had been cleared and there was nothing left to do but go, we stayed and began to share our stories.

All of us had married. Some are still with the fellows we started out with as girls. A few divorced, some have been widowed. All of us have raised children, biological, adopted, or borrowed, and the sound of their names when we talk about them lights up our faces. If there are problems with our kids, now edging into middle age, we don't talk about them over lunch. Mostly, we agree, we've sent good people out into the world to carry on. There's no need to remind each other that this has been no small feat in a society changing at warp speed.

A few of us are great-grandparents. One became a grandmother for the first time two weeks ago. Some of our grandchildren have been adopted from countries on the other side of the world, places so distant in miles and culture from our rural Kentucky childhoods that we have no map to guide us but the heart.

We've earned paychecks, too. We've been bankers, teachers, stewardesses, editors and journalists, nurses, florists, office workers, bookkeepers, poets, gas station and grocery store owners, farmers. We've gone to faraway places, in this country and across the world, that we only read about in books when we were children growing up on Owen County tobacco farms.

We've volunteered in our communities in ways too numerous to name, made a difference in ways that cannot be ignored. We've voted and have been good citizens, taken care of aging parents, ill spouses and siblings, and endured the inevitable decline of our own bodies. We've known grief, disappointment, regret, joy, success, and accomplishment.

"STEEL MAGNOLIAS," SONDRA SAYS as we linger over coffee after finishing our stories, reluctant to let go of each other. Yes, I nod. We're resilient and beautiful, we not-quite-boomers, the last hurrah of the war babies. We have a way of smiling through adversity—our legacy from June Cleaver? And the determination not to break, even when we're creased—the influence of Steinem?

But on this singular August afternoon, we're girls once again. Girls on a summer day.

IN THE GARDEN

THOUGH I'M A GRANDMOTHER NOW, I can slide without warning through Alice's looking glass, where I catch glimpses of the girl I used to be. When the near-forgotten scents of a spring night in May sneak up behind me, when—well, it happened again on Sunday morning, about the time my large congregation of city Methodists hit the chorus of that old gospel hymn, "In the Garden."

From about the eighth grade through the twelfth, I was the pianist at the New Columbus Methodist Church. Don't be impressed. I landed the unpaid job by default. The prior pianists had died or moved away, and although my skill at the keyboard was shaky, no one else in our tiny rural church could tickle the ivories at all. But thanks to Mother's persistence, I could play—sort of. When I was in the third grade, she had signed me up for piano lessons with Mrs. Settle over in Owenton. Though I demonstrated no talent whatsoever, Mrs. Settle was a teacher with stoic resolve and Mother continued to ferry me thirty miles round trip to piano lessons for the next nine years.

When the piano bench went vacant, Mother felt vindicated. "See," she said. "Now you can play hymns for church." It was never clear to me why I would want to do this, but the church was desperate, and pleasing both God and Mother seemed like the right thing to do.

On some level I did not completely understand, I knew that I was pinch-hitting for Mother. She was so tone-deaf that Cousin Mae once asked her to stop singing in the church pew because she was getting everyone around her off key. Like a good Christian should, Mother turned the other cheek, never doing more than humming under her breath in the song service again. It is written, however, that the meek shall inherit the earth. My ascension to the Methodist's piano bench was an advance on Mother's inheritance.

We had no choir, and in my memory, the experienced song leaders kept politely resigning after going a Sunday or two with me at the keyboard. First Mr. Bell bowed out, then Cousin Mae, then someone whose name I've forgotten. Finally, X was drafted into service. Married to a godly woman, he had recently found religion and been saved from a life of drink. "Wouldn't it be a good idea for X to have a leadership position in the church to help keep him from backsliding?" someone asked, and then everyone wondered why they hadn't thought of him before.

Thus, an unlikely worship team was anointed, both of us novices, he an aging, bald-headed tobacco farmer, I a stick of a girl. X could not read music—my only advantage—and he strained when he reached for the high notes. But he sang on key with a pleasing voice within his range, and he brought the fervor of the newly converted to his job.

What X and I lacked in musical finesse, we made up for in volume. With only forty people in attendance on a good day, we felt compelled to compensate for the empty pews by filling the big, old church with joyful noise. *X* sang as loud as he could, and I banged the keys with gusto sort of like I'd heard Jerry Lee Lewis do on the radio, creating a style I thought cleverly merged "Great Balls of Fire" with the *Methodist Hymnal.*

The problem was, I often hit the wrong notes. Dissonant clinkers. When I did, *X* would keep right on going, singing louder to cover me, never letting on that he noticed I'd blundered. Only when I played "In the Garden" did I relinquish my rock 'n' roll act. I could play that hymn tenderly—perfectly—and the lower range of the melody was ideal for *X*'s voice. Oh I wish you could have heard us.

By the time we got hold of "In the Garden," it was already famous, of course. Billy Sunday's tent revivals had made it popular in the early 1900s. By mid-century, it had become a secular favorite, recorded by artists as diverse as Roy Rogers, Perry Como, and Elvis Presley. It even made it into several movie scores. But I'd put our rendition up there with the best of them.

We fell into a pattern. If I were having an especially difficult morning at the keyboard, he'd announce, without missing a beat, that our next number would be "In the Garden."

"I come to the garden alone / While the dew is still on the roses..." I'd breathe a little easier, and we'd move right along as though I had not recently murdered all the onward Christian soldiers.

"And the voice I hear falling on my ear..." He'd sing in his melodious tone, and my hands would stop shaking.

"And the joy we share as we tarry there..." By the end of the first refrain, I would suddenly realize I was enjoying making music. I'd glance at *X*, and he'd be smiling at me with that wide grin of his.

The refrain came round again, *"And He walks with me / And He talks with me / And He tells me I am His own..."* Remarkably, when the morning service was over, X never failed to compliment my less-than-stellar performance and thank me for helping him.

In time, I went off to college and I stopped playing the piano. When his wife passed away, X left his farm for a town somewhere and I never saw him again. I heard a rumor he returned to drinking before he died, but if so, that's not for me to question. I am left only to remember those long-ago Sundays I shared with him when I first began to grasp the meaning of grace.

MR. NICK'S ICE CREAM CONES

IN MY MEMORY, HE RESEMBLED Norman Rockwell's St. Nick on the cover of *The Saturday Evening Post*—if Santa had gotten a shave and maybe a little haircut, too. Bald on top of his head, his remaining white hair wisped wildly wherever it could and his blue eyes twinkled above rosy cheeks. His suspenders stretched tight across his round belly as he bantered with us.

"Yes, we have no banana today!"

Each school day, fifty or more of us schoolkids would crush into his tiny country store at lunchtime, pushing the walls of the shotgun building to its breaking point. Squealing in a single voice that reverberated off the low, pressed-tin ceiling, we demanded bowls of Miz Nick's chili or a steaming hot dog. Satiated and quieter, we would then line up and wait for Mr. Nick to dip our ice cream cones.

Mr. Nick constructed his sugary pyramids with abandon, always talking, rapid-fire, barely pausing to take a breath. He would lean, bent to his waist, to plunge the dipper into the frozen rainbow, his voice warming the freezer as he talked.

"Got a new flavor, you wanna try it, you better try it, wanna try it?"

Then up he would pop with another fat scoop to pack ever deeper, ever tighter, into the cone he balanced in his other hand. When the confection was leaning like the Tower of Pisa, and not a moment sooner, he'd say, "Just a little more," and top it off with one more dollop.

We were the children of tobacco farmers, some of us with enough at home, some with little, a few with less than little. But for a nickel, Mr. Nick handed each of us ethereal abundance—the taste of luxury buried in golden veins of butterscotch ripple or piled high on rich mountains of chocolate.

Had someone told us, we would have understood that ice cream was created to tickle the palates of kings and that Dolley Madison dazzled Washington when she introduced it at White House dinners. Ice cream was, well, downright splendid—and hard to come by. It didn't travel well over the crooked miles that separated our farmhouses from Kroger's frozen food aisle in the county seat.

But then—about 1952, I think—Mr. Nick amazed our isolated, rural community by purchasing a big chest ice cream freezer like the drugstores in town had. He placed it in the rear of his little store, near an equally new black-and-white TV, and welcomed the community to come in and sit a spell on old church pews painted a shiny gray. It was a brilliant business move that would lift his family into relative prosperity not unlike that transforming the rest of postwar America. The traffic in and out of Nick's Grocery boomed, and it became an unofficial community center for the surrounding farms. It was especially busy on Saturday nights, when families would gather to watch whatever might be flashing across the TV screen—wrestling matches or a variety show featuring music or comedians.

Nick's looked like hundreds of other such stores scattered across the rural South in that era. You've likely seen photos of such places. The low-slung building had never been painted, yet it was a colorful sight, covered by metal advertising signs. A concrete porch stretched across the narrow front of the building, and in fair weather, that's where the loafers sat swapping stories. From the porch, over the years, metal caps from Coke bottles had been tossed carelessly onto the parking area, and by my time, hundreds of tires, coming and going, had flattened the little round discs into a solid, paved surface. Inside, the dusty pine floors were held in place by black oil applied annually, and the walls were lined from floor to ceiling with shelves packed with a little bit of everything, from groceries to washcloths to cheap perfume.

Our schoolhouse stood across the one-lane gravel road. Although it was a handsome, stone structure built by the WPA, as I've mentioned before, the school had no central heat or indoor toilets and, of course, no cafeteria. However, we were allowed to run over to Nick's to buy our lunch. Back then, most any Kentucky country store could slice up a sandwich out of the lunch-meat case that would have given a New York City delicatessen a run for the money. Nick's, however, had moved a notch above the others, in our opinion, when it added its makeshift ice cream parlor.

Even as a child, I understood that he was giving us too much for too little. I'm embarrassed that it's taken me a lifetime to ask myself why he did it. At the time, I thought—oh, I don't know what I thought. Maybe that he wanted us kids to like him? But he didn't pay any attention to us unless he was serving up ice cream, and often he was abrupt and impatient with us when we took too long to decide what flavor we wanted. "Hurry up! Hurry up! There's people behind you waiting!" And after all, he had nine kids of his own and who knows how many grandchildren.

Ah—he had nine children of his own. Nine children he had fed from a hardscrabble farm during the Depression in the years before he and Miz Nick opened the store.

And by the time I knew him, he had buried two of them. Billy died at age seventeen of typhoid fever. They lost Bobby when he was three months old to dehydration.

More recently, I've learned that Mr. Nick was a semi-orphan. I'm hazy on the details—he was born in 1895, and who is left to tell me?—but his mother died when he was three, and he was mostly raised by aunts and uncles. I have no reason to think they weren't loving and good to him, but Owen County tobacco sold for a penny a pound at the turn of that century.

Though we can try, from the long distance of time, I realize that it's impossible to understand the whys of another person's life. Time and place combine with chance to shape who we become, and even then, people do not respond in the same way to the same turn of luck, in the same place in the same times. Some become cynical, others become thankful survivors. Some become gentler, others gruff and tougher.

And some never let us catch them looking back on the road they've traveled. They just give away ice cream, because, doggone it, they finally have it to give.

DR. CULL

IN MY LIFETIME, IT'S BEEN EASY to become blasé about miracles. Men walk on the moon, polio exits the conversation, telephones shrink to fit into your pocket, computers take over the world without firing a shot. And you forget that not so long ago, of all the children born, half died of infectious diseases, like strep throat, measles, and pneumonia.

When I was five, I became very sick and, as children will, I became very sick very quickly. We had gone to Uncle Harry's farm on the other side of the county for a celebration of the many family birthdays that fell in December. I was excited about going. An only child, I was always lonely for other children, and my cousin Judy, just my age, would be there. We would play dolls and giggle, and the older cousins would make a fuss over us.

But that afternoon, playing didn't seem as fun as it usually did. The jam cake with the caramel icing didn't taste as good as I remembered either, and I left it uneaten on the plate. All I really wanted, I realized—though it was out of character for me—was a nap. I wandered into the bedroom where the pile of guests' coats had been carefully laid across the bed. I climbed up onto the high mattress and burrowed a warm nest in the middle of the wool garments. By this time, I had begun to feel quite cold.

After that, I don't remember anything until the next day. I awoke back at our house and found myself in my grandfather's large bed in his first-floor bedroom instead of upstairs on my narrow cot. Mother and Daddy and Gran were hovering over me.

Looking at me but talking to Daddy, Mother said, "Go get the new doctor at Corinth." My grandfather, who thought doctors were useful only for setting broken bones, said nothing.

When the doctor arrived (yes, he made house calls), he said little but checked me over thoroughly. "Double pneumonia" was his diagnosis. I can only imagine the terror those words struck in my family's heart.

Then he said, "But a shot of penicillin should fix her up." When he added, "And give her all the Coca-Cola she wants," I fell in love with him.

It was the first penicillin shot anyone in my family had ever had. Although penicillin had played a heroic role late in World War II, in 1950 it was still something most people had only read about. It was only beginning to trickle into the general practice of medicine.

We soon understood why it was called a "miracle drug." Within an hour or so, I felt well enough to get out of bed and play. My grandfather shook his head in bewilderment and delight, and from that day on, he would be the first to insist I see the doctor whenever I was the least bit sick.

Now, the mystery here to me is how the village of Corinth—population perhaps three hundred—had persuaded a *bona fide* doctor, a graduate of an AMA-accredited medical school, to set up shop on its Main Street. Corinth had neither a hospital nor a drugstore.

Its business district consisted of a couple of groceries, a feedstore, a funeral home, a movie theater, and a bank. Admittedly, the Greyhound bus did stop there because US Highway 25 was the major north-south route from Michigan to Florida, and the train paused long enough to whistle.

Corinth, of course, had seen better days. A railroad town, it had been a regional commercial center in the late nineteenth century and well into the twentieth. In 1930, its high school men's basketball team had won third place in the national tournament. Even in 1950, horse pulling contests and softball games continued to draw huge crowds into town on Saturday nights.

I presume, then, that Corinth mustered its civic memories and promised the young doctor everything it could to lure him. Personally, though, I believe God had a hand in leading Dr. Cull into our lives because he would have succeeded in medicine most anywhere.

In the years that followed my bout with pneumonia, Dr. Cull steadied my family through numerous routine illnesses and several major health crises, such as my grandfather's fatal blood disorder and my mother's struggle with kidney disease. Once we fetched him in the middle of the night for Mother. I was too young to understand the particulars of the emergency, but I remember that he told Daddy to take her immediately to a big-city hospital in Lexington. Helping my father get her into the car for the fifty-mile ride, he crawled on his hands and knees into the floor of the back seat to administer medication. "This will get you to the hospital, Mrs. Green." The quiet gentleness in his voice as he said those words has lingered in my memory for the remainder of my life.

When a hospital was built fifteen miles away in the small county seat town of Owenton, Dr. Cull moved his practice there. House calls faded away, but my family continued to "doctor" with him for another thirty-five years, until Daddy's death and Mother's move to Lexington. They considered him "one of the best family doctors in America" and thought his instinct for diagnosis was remarkable. Their opinion was shared by several generations of Owen Countians. I can vouch for his extraordinary memory. Not long before her death, I called him with a question about Mother's medical history, and without referring to her chart, he began to tell me in accurate detail about that long-ago medical problem.

Now I am a grandmother, and Dr. Cull's long life, like my parents' lives, has ended. Looking back, I have a fuller understanding of the sacrifices he made to be a country doctor. I'm unsure why he made the choice to come to us rather than practicing in a larger town. Surely his working hours would have been more humane than they were with us, where he was often the only doctor for miles, and patients would wait in queue to see him until seven or eight in the evening. Surely it might have more gratifying to work in a larger hospital, to have more cutting-edge tools for diagnosis. Surely he would have made more money than he did in a poor area like our pocket of Kentucky, where many people were unable to pay him. Surely it would have been more professionally prestigious, perhaps more intellectually stimulating also, to have plied his trade in a puddle more significant in the world than the rural communities of Corinth and Owenton. Only he could answer that question, but I never thought to ask him, much less thank him.

But I am thankful. I pull my healthy grandbabies close around me and thank Dr. Cull and God for bringing the miracles of modern medicine to me and my family in rural Kentucky.

AN AVERAGE ANGEL

WHEN A PERSON LIVES FOR OVER A HUNDRED YEARS, wits and spirit intact, you forget that they won't live forever. I'd been "laying off," as Daddy used to say, to write about Mrs. Payne for a long time. Then, a little while ago, without warning, she left this earth as quietly, as efficiently, as she had lived.

The real reason I've not written about her before now, of course, is that it's hard to write about an angel without sounding like a Hallmark card. I have no funny stories to tell about Mrs. Payne or courageous feats to record—although facing a classroom of adolescents for a lifetime might qualify as heroism on the front line.

I met Mrs. Payne, a woman already in middle age, when I was a full-of-myself high school senior. When I walked into her World History class the first day of school, I already had one foot out the door on the road to the future. We were not much alike. She was petite and immaculately dressed in pastel suits. I was tall and awkward in madras plaid. She was soft-spoken and even-keeled, I was dramatic and emotional.

But we both liked history. That was a good thing because we commenced at its beginning and worked our way into the twentieth century. Whew. The main thing I remember about the class, however, is that she forgave me my seventeen-year-old arrogance.

In the middle of the second semester, about the time I'd begun to cast myself in the role of class valedictorian, she laid a big assignment on us. She asked us to read an historical novel or nonfiction book of our choice. We were to write a report, of course, but the largest portion of our grade hinged on the oral presentation about the book to the class. Now, remember, I was full of myself—so I chose to read *Doctor Zhivago*.

Only a few years earlier, Boris Pasternak's masterpiece about the aftermath of the Russian Revolution had been smuggled out of the Soviet Union. It was received with great fanfare in the West, and to the dismay of the Communist Party, Pasternak had been awarded the Nobel Prize for Literature. Striking a blow for democracy and standing tall for the Free World, I impressed myself with my selection. I felt intellectually superior to my classmates, who opted for old-school Dickens or Crane's easy-peasy *The Red Badge of Courage*.

The problem with being full of yourself is that Russian novelists don't give a hoot. Pasternak whipped me. His *Doctor Zhivago* is 648 pages long, and its legion of characters—oh, how many, how many— weave in and out of the entire narrative which, to confuse the reader, is divided into loosely connected sections. In the Russian literary tradition, each character also has three different names, which Pasternak uses interchangeably without explanation, first one name then the other, even on the same page.

The night before the oral report was due, I still had a third of the book to finish. I did what any battered Cold War warrior might do—I skimmed the last 250 pages. Of *Doctor Zhivago*! In an era before Google or CliffsNotes!

To say I was nervous when I stood before the class the next day would be an understatement. Mrs. Payne knew instantly that I was in over my head with the good doctor. But when I stumbled to my conclusion, she gave me that look of hers, the kind one with the little smile, the one that forgave. She knew I'd learned something more significant than Boris Pasternak had to say to me.

OVER THE DECADES THAT FOLLOWED, Mrs. Payne stayed in touch with me and made me feel special to her, perhaps even cherished. She'd include a handwritten note in her annual Christmas card, and when I finally published my first book, she was there, looking gorgeous at ninety-one, with her perfect, honey-blonde hair, to hear me read at the library.

At her funeral, though, I realized that she'd made most everyone feel cherished. On a busy Saturday morning, the McDonald & New Funeral Home was packed with people there to pay their final respects to a woman who'd been born over a century earlier. First one and then another said things like, "She looked out for me and made sure I stayed out of trouble after my mother died." "She was such an honorable person, a role model for me." "She wouldn't let you talk about her illnesses or problems but always wanted to know about yours." "She just wouldn't quit doing what needed to be done." "I called her Aunt Verna, but she wasn't my real aunt. I just felt like she was."

As the music began for the funeral, the woman sitting next to me murmured to no one in particular, "She was an icon."

An *icon*—a word with a huge meaning that's been whittled down by sportscasters who've overused it. But when you've met a real icon, you know it. Even if she's a soft-spoken, tiny woman in a pastel suit.

DOWN YONDER IN THE PAWPAW PATCH

I WANTED TO LOVE PAWPAWS. The name enchanted me. One of the earliest nursery rhyme ditties I learned featured this indigenous fruit. *"Way down yonder in the pawpaw patch,"* we'd sing as we skipped in a circle holding hands.

At first I thought we were singing about a patch of grandfathers, an image I loved then and still do. Imagine that—growing a whole field full of doting granddaddies, like you raised tomatoes or tobacco! You see, my clan of Green cousins and I called our grandfather "Pawpaw." Lots of people I knew when I was a child also had beloved Pawpaws.

I've since come to realize this may be only a rural Kentucky thing because my friends from the north are puzzled when I talk about my Pawpaw. Even after I explain that it is a common name given to grandfathers where I come from, they remain befuddled, as though I were translating ancient Sanskrit.

When I learned that Kentucky's answer to bananas was also called a pawpaw, I couldn't wait to eat one. I love bananas, and pawpaws grew free for the picking, I was told. How could it get any better? Unfortunately, the misguided pawpaw (it's a tropical fruit that took a U-turn to nontropical North America, back when time began) is as hard to spot in season as a dodo bird. To paraphrase the lesson Alice learned about jam when she stepped through the looking glass, "The rule is, pawpaws tomorrow and pawpaws yesterday—but never pawpaws today." The mischievous fruit is either underripe or overripe, and its elusive moment of perfection bursts forth at midnight under the first blood moon of—well, you get the idea.

Finally, a year or so after Ernie and I married, my sweet father-in-law carried in a hat full of "perfect" pawpaws from his Kentucky River farm for me to sample. He was a connoisseur of this native delicacy and declared it superior to a banana or a pear—or maybe even your favorite pie, pick a flavor. He stood in their farmhouse kitchen, his hair still full and dark that day, his face younger looking and less wrinkled than mine is now, and extended this precious offering to me with his easy smile. His topaz eyes (why couldn't my children have inherited those?) danced with anticipation as he waited for my reaction. In that moment I understood how much he wanted his pawpaws to impress—no, to *please*—me.

Well.

I bit into the misshapen sort-of-looks-like-a-pear fruit. It tasted like—words fail me. Maybe a *dead* banana? Maybe a tasteless, over-cooked squash? Maybe a vaguely sweet wet wad of paper a kid had chewed on? No, I take that last comparison back because I've since learned that goats refuse to eat pawpaws.

That was the first and last time I ever tasted a pawpaw, but that scene in the kitchen has lingered in my memory for a lifetime. Perhaps that's why an interview with Chris Chmiel on NPR's food blog, *The Salt*, caught my attention. Chmiel has planted his own pawpaw orchard near Athens in southern Ohio. Who knew you could plant pawpaw trees? I thought there was a cosmic rule that they could only grow spontaneously in wild patches.

Chmiel has also founded a Pawpaw Festival, since every self-respecting fruit must have its own. He allows, however, that the festival became more festive once he hit upon a way to make pawpaw beer.

A distant cousin of tropical fruits, the pawpaw inexplicably prefers to hang out with apple, pear, hickory nut, and walnut trees in nontropical regions of America, like Appalachia, or the sort of place where a good river runs through it, like the Ohio, the Mississippi or, as on my in-laws' farm, the Kentucky. Full of protein and vitamins, the pawpaw supposedly sustained members of the Lewis and Clark expedition during a particularly lean stretch of their journey. And Thomas Jefferson once sent some to the ambassador of France. That gesture may explain the disdain the French still maintain for American cuisine.

However, even an eat-local cheerleader like Chmiel admits that it's unlikely pawpaws will ever be sold in your local supermarket. It's the old jam yesterday, jam tomorrow conundrum—pawpaws have only a brief, fleeting moment of desirability. You *can* mash them to make pawpaw bread or jelly, but then the concentrated fruit has a nasty little habit of causing intestinal distress in some folks, what Chmiel alludes to as "the poo-poo issue." (Apparently, people don't care about the poo-poo issue when they drink pawpaw beer.)

But back to my father-in-law. I loved him dearly, and I wanted to love his pawpaws, too. I really did. But though I double-majored in theater in college and am inclined by temperament to be mindful of others' feelings, I could not muster a "pawpaws are divine" look on my face on that long-ago day. The best I could do was a polite verbal response. "Interesting," I said, followed by the old fallback, "certainly different." Then I made a graceful exit to the bathroom in case I really *did* need to vomit.

For the remainder of his life, we never mentioned pawpaws again. I loved him for that, for letting my divergent tastes go unchallenged, unremarked upon, in this and in all things.

Although I never ate another pawpaw, I did teach my children to call their paternal grandfather by that affectionate name. Lucky for them, he and his kind flourished in the uncultivated patches that spread, root sprout to root sprout, down yonder by the Kentucky River.

HOW TO SELECT A GOOD HUSBAND

THE PHONE RANG SOMETIME IN THE DEAD ZONE between midnight and dawn. It may have been the second year we were married, or maybe the third, because I remember we were living in our first house, not the apartment, but we did not yet have children. Later, our who-cares-a-fig-what-time-it-is babies would wreak havoc with our nights, but back then a predawn wake-up call was an extraordinary event.

Actually, Ernie and I still considered the telephone itself an extraordinary event. We both grew up in rural pockets of Owen County, where home telephone service was not available until we were teenagers. A phone call lingered in our psyche as something only a few degrees less demanding of our immediate attention than a telegram. It meant someone was reaching out to us with good news or bad, or to invite us somewhere, or to tell us they were on their way to our house. In an era before answering machines, it did not occur to us to ignore a ringing phone, much less a call in the middle of the night.

So, when it woke Ernie from a sound sleep, he did what came natural to him. He fumbled for the receiver on our bedside table, and in the dark, knocked the alarm clock over in the process. A man's voice asked to speak to me by name.

"Wake up, Georgia," Ernie said. "Somebody needs to talk to you on the phone."

I'm a sound sleeper, and it took a minute or two for me to realize that I was not dreaming. Ernie was, indeed, shaking my shoulder, trying to get me to wake up. Was the house on fire? Was someone trying to break in? No? I have a phone call?

"Yes," he said. "Here, take the phone."

And so I did. In a serious voice, the man asked if he were speaking to Georgia Stamper. As the knot began to form in my stomach, I assured him he was. Mother kept my phone number in her billfold as her emergency contact. Had my parents, who lived hours away, been in an accident? Were they lying unconscious in a hospital somewhere? Were they dead?

But no. In my half-asleep, panicked state of mind, it took me about a minute to realize that the man's words were becoming more and more—erotic. I'd been the target of an obscene phone call, likely from one of my teenage students.

At first I was irked at Ernie. Then I thought it was funny, and his "waking me to take a you-know-what kind of call" became an entertaining story that we laughed about with friends. Much later, I understood that I had married a man who was both confident and trusting. It's a special kind of guy, after all, who will wake up his wife in the middle of the night to take a call from a strange man without a question to either of us.

Over a lifetime, I've also come to appreciate how special it is to have a husband who answers the phone when *I* call. During his years working for a large corporation, Ernie put in long hours and often traveled throughout the country and the world. He was never more than a phone call away, however, regardless of the hour, regardless of the miles, regardless of the relative unimportance of my problem.

He also answers the phone whenever any of our family or friends need him. One December night, for example, our daughter called him about nine o'clock. Just a few miles north of Knoxville, she was driving home to Lexington from the University of South Carolina for Christmas break. At the midway point in her long quest for a terminal graduate degree, she'd had little sleep for weeks as she wrote paper after paper and prepared for exams. In tears, she allowed as how she couldn't stay awake to drive a minute longer. I would have said, "Get a motel room, and start again tomorrow." But hearing the yearning to be home in her voice, Ernie said, "I'll come to you and drive your car back to Lexington." Within fifteen minutes, he and her sister took off to fetch her home to Kentucky.

That response is typical of how Ernie has responded to calls over a lifetime. Sometimes they've been important, related to issues in his work life or a crisis for a friend or family member. However, he's been as obliging to the calls that were less urgent. A technical question about a computer issue, a photograph he once shot that someone wants to copy, a genealogical question, a grandchild's request to be motored from one school activity to another, a daughter or friend's request for a favor—Ernie answers the phone politely and helps if he possibly can. Stephen Covey's seven-step guide to success might not approve of Ernie's "all calls are equal" approach to life, but then success is defined differently by each of us.

Now that technology has plunged us into a brave new world, I have convinced him that it's okay not to answer an unknown number and that he does not have to be polite to human voices that are computer generated. Still, if I were interviewed on the secret to selecting a good husband, my advice would be simple. Marry a man who will answer the phone.

AUNT HELEN'S CAST-IRON SKILLET SPAGHETTI

I DON'T KNOW WHERE AUNT HELEN FOUND IT, maybe on the back of a box of Creamette pasta. More likely, she invented it out of necessity. But she whipped up a batch of cast-iron skillet spaghetti every week, like a repetitive pep talk, from the beginning of November until daffodils bloomed. Other family cooks followed her lead.

I admit that we grew a little tired of it before the weather lifted. Sometimes you'd yearn instead for out-of-season strawberries floating in yellow cream or for an escape to a southern beach to taste the exotic unexperienced. To be honest, sometimes you just wanted to give up. But Aunt Helen didn't hold with giving up, and her recipe reminded us that constancy can—and usually will—prevail.

A one-dish meal cooked on top of the range, cast-iron skillet spaghetti's ingredients were standard: onion, hamburger, tomatoes, a plethora of spices. It took a U-turn away from classic Italian spaghetti, however, when you plunged dry, broken pasta into the bubbling mixture. Covered, it simmered then for an hour, presumably to allow the noodles to mush up and soak in the sauce. I believe the real reason was to give the tantalizing aroma time enough to float throughout the house, coaxing the weariness from our bones and spirits.

Such a recipe wouldn't be trendy with today's foodies, but Aunt Helen didn't hold much with trendy. She wasn't tolerant of vices like drinking or sleeping in on Sunday morning and skipping church. She wasn't much bothered by teenage "sensitive feelings," if our makeup and clothes didn't conform to a neat, ladylike appearance. By today's standards, she might be considered too opinionated—if having specific ideas about standards makes one opinionated.

But she always had a new joke that made me laugh, and she laughed at mine. She rooted passionately for the University of Kentucky basketball team, and she could be ready on short notice to take a trip if you had an itch to go somewhere. Aunt Helen was a lot of fun.

She was also good. Plain old, cast-iron, everyday good—like her spaghetti. If I could, I would make her kind a protected species before they become extinct. The bad tend to make for more interesting stories in literature and get more than their share of words (and, in real life, too often more than their share of wealth, fame, and power). However, heroes who do extraordinary feats get their due, also. It seems to me, though, that the efforts of ordinary, day in and day out, good people like Aunt Helen too often get overlooked, in both literature and life.

She was the anonymous person who treated all the children to an ice cream cone on every field trip. If you needed an elusive doodad tracked down and purchased, or someone to help Pawpaw Green buy and wrap fifty Christmas gifts for his sprawling family, Aunt Helen quietly did it.

When you needed someone to clap for you, Aunt Helen showed up. When you needed someone to sit beside you in the hospital, she was there. When you sank to your knees in discouragement,

Aunt Helen would stop by with a pie and hold your hand. When you thought you couldn't take another step, Aunt Helen was there, without fanfare or fuss, doing whatever little thing needed to be done to help you keep going on.

She quite simply loved us all, without jealousy, without explanation. The youngest of my father's six siblings, she was the linchpin that held together my Green relatives.

"Pshaw," (or some variation of that word) she'd say, if she were living. "I haven't done anything worth talking about." Her modesty had been shaped in childhood, when she (wrongly) concluded she wasn't as pretty as her sister or as smart as her brainy brothers. Maybe that's when she decided that the thing she could do better than the others was to prop us up.

During World War II, she left rural Kentucky to follow her sailor husband to New York City. She found a place to live, an office job in Manhattan, and learned to navigate the subway and winter street corners in a thin wool coat.

In November of 1945, when her daughter was only ten days old, Aunt Helen hopped a train from New York City and brought her newborn baby and her exhausted, postwar seaman back to Kentucky. A lifetime later, when I asked how she was physically able to make the trip, she laughed in her familiar way, dismissing my question. When I kept pressing her, she finally said, "I wanted to get home. You do what you have to do."

She'd told me that before, I realized, in example of course, but in words, too. During my childhood, when my mother was extremely ill, she and my uncle drove me to the Lexington hospital to visit her. We made the long trip home to Owen County very late that night, and I could not hold my eyes open. "How can Uncle stay awake to drive us?"

I wondered out loud. Her answer rings clear, still: "You don't quit when you have a job to do."

She had the mild misfortune of looking exactly like her father, my Pawpaw Green. His rangy frame and craggy features made for an effortlessly imposing man, but Aunt Helen, who became a fine-looking woman, had to work to make the best of them. For example, she inherited his unusually large earlobes, so I never saw her, even working in her kitchen, without sizable, clip-on earrings. Clairol talked her dishwater hair into strawberry blonde. Tall and angular to the edge of boney, she had the last laugh on her curvy peers, maintaining her weight—to the pound—from high school to Medicare.

Images of her float through my memory. I reach out to touch her large, square hands so like my own, and she glides away from me, laughing at one of her jokes. Perhaps I leaned on her so much because she was an extension of Mother, her best friend. Perhaps it was because I was an only child, seeking to expand the tiny circle of my immediate family. Perhaps our personalities just clicked, a mysterious blend of shared DNA.

I thought she'd live to be a hundred, as the Greens often do. I'd visit her three times a week in the nursing home and repay her with new jokes for the million times she'd made me laugh, for the million times she'd wiped my tears. I would be the devoted niece repaying her with love and attention for all she had done for me, for everyone.

Instead, she fell in action, frying chicken to feed our grieving family an hour after she learned of the unexpected death of her young niece. Still as straight and limber as she'd been in high school, she simply dropped from worry about us, I believe.

When family found her on the floor, she ordered someone to fetch her a clean pair of slacks from the closet to wear in the ambulance.

Because a clean, neat appearance matters, you know, even when you've had a stroke! Within minutes of struggling into the fresh trousers, she was gone.

IT'S NOVEMBER AGAIN, time for Aunt Helen's cast-iron skillet spaghetti, and I realize I've misplaced her recipe. I'm left to muddle through the rainy season with problems leaking through every crevice of my life, with only the memory of Aunt Helen and her spaghetti. Maybe that's enough.

SHEPHERDS IN BATHROBES

WHEN I WAS A CHILD, I thought the Three Wise Men and the Shepherds really had worn bathrobes and black socks when they came to adore the Christ Child. This was the way they were always dressed in the Christmas pageant at our church, and I assumed the costuming was historically accurate. I wasn't quite sure why biblical men had wrapped terrycloth towels around their heads, but since Christmas is often cold in Kentucky, I figured they probably wanted to keep their bald heads warm.

Our tiny Methodist church thought big, and we staged an elaborate reenactment of the Christmas story every year (although the director made an annual announcement that she would never do this again). To pull this off, everyone in the congregation was drafted into service. Even the youngest served as stable animals, and the most elderly turned the light switches on and off at critical moments. Were it not for the kindness of the Baptists across the road, we would have played to empty pews. We cast them as the audience, and they obliged by dismissing their Sunday night service to help us out.

I can still recall the angels' wings. They were shaped out of baling wire from the hayfield and then were covered, from span to span, with multiple layers of ivory crepe paper. A creative, genial woman, who died much too young, tediously shaped the overlapping layers of fragile paper into thousands of feather-like ruffles. The wings were magnificent, and I'm pretty sure God added Margaret Carr's design to his pattern book.

Our choir of angels who sang on high was small, but their voices were fine and pure and covered every part. Mr. and Mrs. Bell could not be equaled at bass and alto, Cousin Mae hit the soprano notes with the skill of a trained opera singer, Bill (who later became a Baptist but got his start in the Methodist choir) sang a fine tenor, and his future wife, Faye, handled the keyboard with skill. There were a few other angels, too—even me—but mostly we only hummed.

Mrs. P. was the perennial director and, in real life, she was a fifth-grade schoolteacher accustomed to being obeyed. Every year, about halfway through the month of rehearsals, she would have a mild breakdown, alternately crying and yelling, because no one was listening to her. Once she spoke sharply to a Wise Man who'd been hastily recruited to fill a bathrobe from the ranks of loitering boyfriends hanging around the Methodist Youth Fellowship. Admittedly, he was flirting when he should have been following yonder star, but he was so taken aback at being reprimanded that he vowed never to darken the door of a church again. I hope he didn't keep that vow—I'd hate to think our Christmas pageant sent him straight to Hell.

Years later, though, whenever I found myself standing in the midst of pandemonium, trying to lead people who did not want to be led (have you ever tried to build gingerbread houses with twenty Girl Scout Brownies in a small room?) I would think about Mrs. P.

and carry on for her sake. I wish I'd told her, when I could, how much the pageants meant to me. One memory, in particular, remains vivid.

Our Shepherds were no-nonsense farmers, recruited from the Adult Men's Sunday School Class. I can only imagine how their Christian faith was tested when they were asked to don ridiculous-looking bathrobes in public, wrap towels around their heads, and come to play practice every Sunday afternoon. To compound their stage misery, one year Mrs. P. surprised the Shepherds at our first rehearsal by altering their perennial silent tableau. This Christmas, the Shepherds would have lines to recite, she said. Then she instructed the Shepherds to move forward one by one and read their assigned paragraphs.

When Shepherd Number Two was called upon, he gamely stepped up. He read the first word, "The," but then stopped. He looked at the floor. He cleared his throat. In an instant, I understood. Shepherd Number Two could not read, at least not well. He was one of the most honorable, pleasant men I've ever met, hardworking and capable, too. I'm sure that in today's schools he would have been diagnosed with dyslexia or some other synapse glitch that made reading more difficult for him than for others. But in that awful moment, he stood mute on the altar of the church.

That's when the good thing happened. Without a look passing between them, the other Shepherds began to read the lines for him, their tongues turned to silver, and then they seamlessly moved on to their own. The Wise Men joined in, too. I've never heard a choral reading more deftly executed. The powerful rhythm of their conjoined voices erased all embarrassment, and we went on to have the best rehearsal we ever had. By the next Sunday, Shepherd Number Two had memorized his lines, and the incident was never spoken of.

So it came to pass that I learned the true meaning of Christmas from farmers wearing bathrobes, with towels on their heads. Whenever I find myself uncertain of my performance in life, I think about those good men—unsure of themselves, too, but unafraid to look ridiculous in the trying.

BUDAPEST ANGELS

ERNIE BROUGHT THE THREE LITTLE ANGELS home from Budapest, Hungary, in 1988—one for each of our daughters, but really a gift for me. Every Christmas season, I carefully unwrap the umber-colored ceramic figures as though they were priceless museum pieces, although he paid only a few dollars for them. About four inches tall, the monochromatic angels kneel with their hands folded in prayer. I place them on a conspicuous tabletop and try to call attention to them by surrounding them with fresh greenery, but they are rarely noticed in our holiday house filled with lights, glitter, and strident red ribbon. But I notice them, and I remember.

Ernie, his boss, and several other colleagues were in Vienna on a business trip and were delighted to find themselves with a free-from-work Sunday. And so his boss decided to engage a tour guide to drive the small group across the Austrian border into Hungary in a seven-passenger van.

At that time, the metaphoric Iron Curtain remained very real to

Americans. Traveling from a Western European country into one in the Communist-controlled Eastern Bloc was not casually undertaken, sometimes not even possible. However, the old order of the Communist world was changing more than we then understood. In 1989, the Berlin Wall would abruptly and unexpectedly come down. In 1991, the Soviet Union itself would collapse. All Ernie and his friends knew that October day in 1988, however, was that it was permissible for them to enter Hungary as tourists for the day. They seized the opportunity to visit the old and storied city of Budapest.

From the outset of the trip, they were a bit uneasy about their driver. With no legal limit, traffic moved at an excessive rate of speed along the flat and very wide two-lane highway connecting Vienna and Budapest. By some understood but undefined rule, cars would part to allow others to pass in the middle, traveling in either direction. Their Turkish chauffeur barreled down the Autobahn on the offense, passing nearly all other drivers, as though daring the smaller vehicles to challenge his GM van, with its V-8 engine.

Nevertheless, they arrived safely in Budapest on one of those perfect days unique to October. The temperature was neither too hot nor too cold. The autumn light fell at a slant across the Danube River and cast Budapest's ornate, old buildings in a soft, mellow hue. They dined at an enchanting outdoor café. Finally, they visited the architecturally magnificent Matthias Church with its multicolored roof—the latter a work of art in itself.

A street fair featuring local artisans was in full swing that afternoon in the plaza surrounding the ancient church. Ernie purchased the three angels from one of the vendors and was intrigued that he *insisted* on being paid in dollars rather than in Hungarian tender. Ernie wondered that afternoon if the artist's illegal eagerness to be paid in American money signaled a shift in the Communist countries. His hunch, of course, would be proven accurate within the next year or so.

En route back to Vienna, but still a long way from the Austrian border, the Kentuckians' happy excursion imploded. A tiny family car—probably the small Yugo which was popular in Europe in the 1980s—abruptly made a U-turn in front of them. Their van was traveling at ninety to one hundred miles per hour, but the driver skillfully managed to slow it. Still, his heroic effort fell short. Their big GM van T-boned the minicar and crushed it like a pop can.

Everyone in Ernie's van was injured, but they soon determined that no one was seriously hurt. Even Ernie's ceramic angels had survived the crash. The couple and child in the car they had hit, however, would have to be extracted with jaws of life. Ernie thought they were dead.

While their Turkish driver spoke German well and spoke enough English to get by, he did not speak a word of the Hungarian language. Neither, of course, did Ernie or anyone in his group. The police arrived and took possession of their passports. Fear crept into the van as the Kentuckians took stock of their situation—Americans in a Communist country, involved in a fatal accident.

Traffic backed up for miles in either direction. Firemen came. More policemen came. Time passed slowly.

And then the angel came. She was a Hungarian nurse married to a doctor, and they were medical missionaries in Nigeria. On this particular day, however, they happened to be home in Hungary, driving down the Autobahn. Miracle of miracles, she spoke fluent English.

In quick order, she determined that the passengers in the squashed tiny car were not dead and somehow had even escaped life-threatening injuries. She attended to the wounds that those in Ernie's group had sustained. Then, significantly, she approached the Hungarian police with bravado and insisted that they get these Americans back to Vienna! To Ernie's amazement, she prevailed.

The police began to flag every tour bus that crept by to see if it had vacant seats to accommodate them. Finally, one did. Grateful to her, Ernie slipped the angel his card and said, "If you are ever in America..."

Six years later, an Ashland Inc. colleague phoned Ernie at his office. She had an odd story to share, she said. Her step-grand-mother, who lived in Lexington, had been rushed to the hospital with a heart attack. Traumatized, the elderly woman had reverted to her native Hungarian language. Unable to communicate with her, the hospital staff had sought assistance from Lexington's international community. Immediately, a woman who spoke fluent Hungarian rushed to the hospital to translate and to calm the stricken elderly woman.

Ernie's colleague had made the two-hour trip from Ashland to the Lexington hospital to visit her step-grandmother as soon as possible. She, of course, profusely thanked the Hungarian stranger for her assistance and learned in conversation that the woman's husband had accepted a research position at the University of Kentucky a year or so earlier.

When Ernie's friend explained that she lived in Ashland and worked for Ashland Inc., the Hungarian got a quizzical look on her face. She dug through her billfold and took out Ernie's old business card. "Do you know this man?" she asked.

AMID THE GLITZ OF THE HOLIDAYS, I continue to make a place for my little praying figurines every Christmas. They go largely unnoticed by visitors who come and go at our home during the season, but they keep me from forgetting that I may entertain angels unawares.

CHRISTMAS EVE

MY MOTHER SPOKE TO ME for the last time on Christmas Eve. I suppose, for some, such a memory might cast a pall on Christmas forever after, but the events of that evening cause me to hold the season closer.

You have to understand that I was Mother's only child and that she synchronized the beating of her heart with my happiness. You have to understand how much effort she put into selecting the perfect Christmas gift for me each year and for everyone else on her list, too. You have to understand how special Christmas Eve was to our family...

My childhood world was split into two parts. Half of the population, maybe less, celebrated the birth of Jesus on Christmas Eve, and the other half, maybe more, on Christmas Day. My family belonged to the Christmas Eve believers, and like most sectarians, I grew up thinking our way was a little better.

The reasons my people held with Christmas Eve have been lost to history. I suspect it had to do with impatience. All I know for sure is that roughly a hundred years ago my maternal grandparents started the tradition of a six o'clock Christmas Eve feast, followed by the opening of gifts around the tree. The extended family would gather and celebrate until midnight. My mother continued her parents' ways. Even Santa cooperated, silently dropping my toys off early out in the barn while we ate supper.

The days leading up to Christmas Eve were like a sappy holiday movie script—except it was for real and Mother had the starring role. Christmas shopping required a fifty-mile trip to Lexington, where she gushed over the displays of twinkling lights and the singing chipmunks in Stewart's Department Store window. Then, no matter how cold it was—in my memory it was always near zero—she would tramp up and down Main Street searching for the right gifts. Mother was an endurance Christmas shopper, not a sprinter. Beginning at Purcell's, which stood about where Rupp Arena does today, she'd trudge to the far end of Main to Wolf Wile, located in what is now the Gray Construction Company Building, and then back and forth a time or two until she met her self-imposed standards for perfect gifts.

She would persuade Daddy to drive us miles over crooked roads to glimpse a live nativity scene at Bethlehem, Kentucky. She would sing holiday songs in her awful voice—the only time of year she would sing—and create treats, like moist blackberry jam cake.

But the climax of the show was the Christmas Eve feast. Its methodically planned menu required a cross-country jaunt to the largest supermarket around to locate hard-to-find items. On our return, Mother would begin cooking. The "old" ham was placed in a lard can and baked to tender perfection overnight. The salads—congealed, frozen, and fruit—could also be put together the day before. Christmas Eve Day was spent roasting the turkey, prepping traditional dishes, like mashed potatoes, and new-fangled ones, like steamed cauliflower with cheese sauce. And our family's recipe for soufflé-like dressing took a lot of attention.

At five-thirty, our guests would arrive, the uncles and aunts, the cousins. At exactly six o'clock, we'd sit down in a roomful of laughter at the mahogany dining room table spread with the best dishware we owned.

There came a time, though, when the party passed to my house. Plagued by glaucoma that compromised her vision and by severe arthritis, Mother was no longer able to host. But she never let go of her excitement about Christmas Eve, and she continued to fret over her gifts, especially her gift to me.

IN OCTOBER OF 2006, Mother was diagnosed with ovarian cancer. It's a silent disease, often undetected until an advanced stage, and this was Mother's situation. In November, she had surgery and the doctor said the cancer was even more invasive than he'd expected. He warned me she had only weeks to live. In early December, I took her home as she asked me to do and tried to make her comfortable.

On December 21, Mother fell into a deep sleep and I could not rouse her. I moved her then to a hospice bed in a local hospital and began praying she would not die on Christmas Eve.

At exactly six o'clock on December 24, the hour our family had sat down for Christmas dinner for a century, she woke up for the first time in three days.

"It's Christmas Eve," she said, with her usual authority. "I have to get up." Euphoric, I rang for nurses to help me lift her. My husband found Christmas carols on his computer and a nurse pulled a Charlie

Brown tree from a hospital storage closet. Then, spooning vanilla ice cream from Dixie Cups, we began our Christmas Eve dinner.

For an hour or more, we sat and talked like we always had. Lucid as ever, she asked about each of my children and my grandchildren. After a while, Mother said she thought she should lie back down.

She never woke up again. We buried her on New Year's Day.

So maybe I believe in prayer and Christmas miracles. Maybe I believe a mother's love transcends death. I do know this for certain. My mother's last Christmas gift to me was perfect.

My Small Acreages

THE CEDARS OF OWEN COUNTY

Juniperus virginiana L.
Eastern red cedar, Virginia juniper

THE CEDARS OF OWEN COUNTY don't hang out with the Cedars of Lebanon. The latter are tree royalty, celebrated in poetry, history, and religion. "God's Cedars," as they're often called, are majestic specimens that can live to be three thousand years old. They raised the Temple in Jerusalem and the palaces of Kings David and Solomon. They sailed the Phoenicians' ships and steadied the rails of the Ottoman Empire. The likes of Queen Victoria took measures to protect the slow-growing trees, and in 1998, the Cedars of God were added to the UNESCO list of World Heritage Sites.

The Cedars of Owen County, however, are only distant cousins—New World mongrels conceived on the wrong side of the sheets.

Technically, they're Virginia junipers, called that because Roanoke colonists were the first to run across them. They share some characteristics with God's Cedars—they're rot- and insect-resistant, for example. But let one slip into your pasture in the spring, and by fall your hillside will sprout with hundreds of its party-crashing buddies.

Yes, the Virginia junipers are scrappy, invasive trees—almost weeds—and can make a go of it in many parts of the United States. However, like my people have done for two centuries, they breathe easiest in the hills of the Outer Bluegrass.

Here, if left alone, they can grow as tall as ninety feet and live up to three hundred years. Stately old cedars mark the burial sites of our early settlers. Dark and dense, they tower beside nineteenth-century houses, like my Uncle Dick Hudson's, and guard isolated, clapboard churches on near-forgotten country roads.

But mostly it's their young we pay attention to because they run wild on the roadsides and over our hills. When they're young, while their figures still curve gracefully into arrowhead-shaped pyramids, they look a lot like Christmas trees are expected to look. They're not ideal for this job. They lack many of the merits of the storied Christmas pines you see in magazines. But pines don't grow wild in the Eden Shale belt of the Outer Bluegrass. Cedars are what we had on our farm when I was a child, and they were free but for the cutting.

We would go out on the hillsides of our farm on a mid-December afternoon, into the gray drizzle and cold, my father with his ax, I with high hopes of finding the perfect Christmas tree. We never did.

Some were too short. Some were too tall or too wide. Some were too brown. Others would look full on one side but lopsidedly sparse on the other. None had the top Daddy sought, strong enough to hold our shiny, metal star.

After an hour, with our toes gone numb in the damp December chill, we'd get less persnickety. "Can we make this one work with a little pruning?" Daddy would ask. "Yes," I'd say, eager by then to return to the warmth of the house and to hot chocolate.

And we always did make it work, even if Daddy had to cut three feet off the bottom to get it into the living room.

"Wonder why it looked smaller in the field?" I'd ask.

We always had to manufacture an artificial pointed top out of baling wire to hold the star.

And, of course, the cedar's prickly yet frail, lacy branches wouldn't hold ornaments like the trees I saw on Christmas cards. We solved that problem by dispensing with ornaments, which we didn't have anyway. Instead, we added popcorn garlands or lightweight tinsel icicles.

Then Mother would pull out a can of aerosol spray snow to cover up the brown foliage.

"I wonder why it looked so much greener in the field?" I'd ask.

In the end, however, our homegrown Christmas tree never disappointed me. The fragrance of the fresh-cut cedar, so moist, so pungent it tickled our throats, took over our small house. With "Silent Night" playing on my transistor radio, I would lie on the floor under the boughs and look up through the starry lights on the feathery branches, until I imagined I glimpsed Bethlehem and Baby Jesus. In the days leading up to Christmas Eve, wrapped packages would appear under its branches, too, and the tree with its loving promises filled me with wonder.

IN TIME, I GREW UP, married, and moved to the pine-covered mountains of Eastern Kentucky. Still, I insisted we have an Owen County Cedar for our first Christmas tree. When we made our Thanksgiving visit to the farm, Ernie cut a fresh cedar and carted it two hundred miles on top of our little Ford Mustang back to our apartment in Ashland.

I can't remember when we started buying one of those mountain pines from the Jaycees lot on the corner because, well, it made more sense. And of course, the pines had pointed tops for the star and limbs stiff enough to hold the ornaments I'd begun to collect.

Nor can I remember when we gave up on a fresh tree altogether and bought an artificial one because, well, it made more sense. We could put it up earlier, and it wouldn't be a fire hazard if we forgot to water it.

Still, the Cedars of Owen County remain my vision of what Christmas trees should be. Sentiment influences me, but I admire the way they volunteer to hold damaged, despairing land in place, saving it from being washed away. Millennia removed from the grandeur of King David's palace, they take root wherever they're sent, tended only by sun and rain. I've even seen them growing out of rock, from ledges of limestone on highway cutaways, as if to offer me encouragement in impossible situations.

So no, they're not royal trees like the Cedars of Lebanon. Like me, they're ordinary commoners—but God's Cedars all the same.

A TOBACCO KIND OF CHRISTMAS

FOR A HUNDRED YEARS, MAYBE TWO HUNDRED, my Owen County family relied on growing tobacco for their economic health. Of course, they did not know how unhealthy smoking was for their bodies, but even understanding that as I do now, I am stunned that within a handful of years, six-bent barns have come to stand empty. Fertile fields lie fallow. And the mammoth tobacco auction warehouses that once dominated towns like Carrollton, Cynthiana, and Lexington have become, like dinosaurs, extinct overnight.

My childhood memories of Christmastime intertwine with the tobacco market like conjoined twins, making it difficult for me to separate one from the other. The *Sears Wish Book* would arrive the week after Thanksgiving, and I would sit, then, in a corner of the stripping room, with its colored pictures spread on my lap, while my parents worked twelve-hour days to make my wishes come true. Preparing the tobacco for market was the next-to-final step in an economic process that had begun in the early spring.

The final step, of course, was selling the tobacco. My family usually opted to take our crop to Lexington, which claimed to be the largest burley tobacco market in the world. I have no reason to think the chamber of commerce was exaggerating. All over town, gigantic auction warehouses came right up to the edge of busy thoroughfares, like South Broadway and Fourth Street—a visual statement of the enormous economic impact tobacco held for Lexington businessmen, as well as the region's farmers.

Now the old warehouses have been torn down or gentrified into loft apartments. Tobacco has become a villain, and few mourn the demise of the auction and government price support system that sustained it. The tobacco warehouses and auctions linger only in footnotes and in the memories of farm kids like me.

THE BURLEY TOBACCO MARKET (not to be confused with North Carolina's flue-cured market) opened in early December on a date calculated to be the coldest of the year. The cavernous buildings were walled with cheap sheets of tin that did little more than infuriate the wind, and a damp chill oozed up through the concrete floors until feet went numb and the roots of the hair on the head froze stiff.

Despite the frigid temperatures, excitement electrified us when we heard the auctioneer's rapid-fire chant echo off the high rafters. He moved up and down the mile-long aisles stacked with dry, brown tobacco, pausing only a few moments at each person's crop. We held our breath when he finally came to our baskets—which were not exactly baskets but woven pallets that cupped shoulder-high hills of crisp tobacco "hands," small bundles of leaves neatly tied together. A year's work hung in the balance of a single minute. Our hearts beat so loud we couldn't be sure of the agreed-on price as the auctioneer, speaking in his rapid, near-foreign language, moved on to sell another family's sweat and tears to the highest bidder.

Only then could we rush forward to see the sale price the buyer had written on the tag.

Only then could we leave the rank-smelling place.

The odor of the dried tobacco leaves was so intense in those warehouses that it cannot be described in olfactory terms. It was something more than smell, a strident presence that seemed to take on three-dimensional shape, like a beam holding up the roof. Or it could have been a living thing, an aggressive virus that invaded our nostrils, settling deep into our lungs. We ran from it as we left the warehouse and drank in the crisp outdoors to purge ourselves, as thirsty for clean, cold air as we had been for ice water in the August fields.

Euphoria welled within us as we drove downtown, where the fine stores lined up along Main Street. We would spend freely for one time during the year, on Christmas gifts and small luxuries, a new electric Mixmaster for my mother or maybe a transistor radio for me. We would eat at Walgreens Drugstore—the "all you can eat" fried fish in a basket was always my choice—or at Purcell's Department Store's more genteel cafeteria, with its fancy fruit salads and fluffy desserts.

Years later, I would learn that the Woolworth's I thought was so wonderful really *was* wonderful, a magnificent example of art deco architecture. Ditto for the Kentucky and Ben Ali movie theaters. I would learn that the Phoenix Hotel, with its canopy that stretched from door to street, its uniformed doormen, and its thick-carpeted lobby, was a pretty good version of a first-class hotel found anywhere.

Lowenthal's fur-filled windows and Embrys vestibule, heavy with the scent of an expensive perfume, were as hoity-toity as shops I'd later see in much larger cities in other parts of the world.

But the burley warehouses that dominated the city's streetscape were unique to Kentucky, even as the tobacco fields that defined the countryside were unique. Drafty temples of commerce, the ware-houses anchored an economic system that was nigh on a religion, sustaining a tribe of people and the land they loved.

Now Lexington's old warehouses are gone, and the fields on our Owen County farm have not grown tobacco for over a decade. Little girls don't sit and dream with the *Sears Wish Book* on their lap, watching their parents prepare the crop for the December market. A tobacco kind of Christmas lingers only in the memories of people like me.

JANUARY IN KENTUCKY

JANUARY IN KENTUCKY REMINDS ME of a difficult relative. You know the kind I mean, the eccentric ones you put up with because you've known them all your life, shared the good times and the bad, and so you love them. But why, oh why, can't they have a better disposition? If she tried harder, couldn't January learn a thing or two from a Bluegrass May or June?

I make myself look for the good in her. She is, I remember, not as mean spirited as her sister in Minnesota, and I do enjoy our fireside chats. But around here, January defines the phrase "drama queen." One day she throws snowballs at us and tries to start a fight. The next night she has a temper tantrum and slaps all the roads with sheets of black ice. Mostly, though, she wallows in despair, raining histrionic tears on the state until we forget the color of the sky. Our lawns and feedlots turn into mud pits that are the envy of the World Wrestling Federation. I've tried to tell her that nobody ever writes songs about a *wet* and *muddy* winter wonderland, but I can't stop her raindrops from falling.

She has a mean streak, too. Why else does she invite the flu and the vomiting runs to come on over and watch a little basketball with us? And don't even get me started on her fascination with pneumonia. Who in their right mind would invite a known killer like Big P to drop by for Sunday dinner?

And while I hate to criticize appearance, January in Kentucky is one ugly month. Oh sure, once in a while she struts. She can throw an ermine stole of snow over her shoulder and look like nature's answer to Marilyn Monroe. And when she brings out the bling in an ice storm, she makes the late Elizabeth Taylor's diamond collection look dowdy. Most of the time, though, she slops around in dull brown or gray, as though she doesn't have enough energy to pull on anything more than a dirty old sweat suit.

And makeup? Forget that, too. The trees are bare and ashen looking, the grass a faded beige, the color of flowers only a memory in seed catalogs. Even the red berries of December have long since been devoured by starving birds, the ones too dumb to pack up and leave for a winter tour of the South.

I guess that latter group would include me, too. Why don't I cut January in Kentucky out of my life and spend the winter in Florida, like so many of my friends do? I'm not sure. The grandchildren are here, for one thing, and then there is the expense of a second home in another state. I don't fish or boat or golf or play tennis. Oh, and my skin doesn't tan. I can't pull off the Florida look.

And then, leaving January behind in Kentucky would make me feel a little disloyal, sort of like walking out on an old friend when she needs me. The truth is, we've been through a lot together over a lifetime. When I carried my parents to their graves on cold winter days, and then a dear friend, and then another and another, she didn't rush my weeping. She listened through the long, dark nights and gave me time to heal.

When I think about it, I realize that time is what Kentucky January has always brought to our relationship. She is more tolerant of my need to slow down than the rest of the calendar seems to be. I don't have to pretend to be someone I'm not, either, that I enjoy skiing or ice-skating or snowshoeing, as those folks up north have to do. I don't have to learn to fish or whatever people do in Florida. She simply lets me be.

No, Kentucky January lets me get away with doing almost nothing for days at a time. I think a little and plan some, make a few lists, stream a movie on TV, or read some books. So mostly I do nothing, and she lets me get away with it because, you know, the weather's lousy outside. There's a little something to be said for a month like that, even if she is neurotic.

DROUGHT

IT HIT 103 DEGREES IN OUR DRIVEWAY TODAY, and I don't have the energy left to muster an exclamation point. Hot's novelty, folks, has worn off. Here in Kentucky, we're moving into the tenth consecutive day of a record-breaking heat wave. Our grass has lost its will to live, and Ernie and I spend our days carrying handfuls of water to the ferns on the deck. "Hang on," we whisper, "hang on."

The people who know about these things keep referring to previous records set in the 1930s and in the 1950s. I wasn't surprised at the statistics cited from the '30s. After all, I've read Steinbeck's *The Grapes of Wrath*. But I didn't realize that the scorched Kentucky summers of my childhood in the 1950s were outside the ordinary.

The heat was only part of the story, though. A "severe drought" hit the state in June 1952 and didn't lift until—are you ready for this?—sometime late in 1955. In fact, meteorologists have named this the "Drought of 1952–1955." Let me say that it was a shock to learn that a hundred-year drought was named for a big chunk of my childhood. Back then, I was oblivious, busy being a kid, but the weather statistics explain some of my memories.

I remember Daddy, a quiet, calm man, pacing on the front porch in an agitated state one afternoon about 1954 or 1955. He raised his arms to the cloudless blue that covered the farm and begged the sky for rain in a voice loud enough for all the angels in Heaven to hear. I'd never seen him or anyone do something like that before, and I felt scared.

After that dramatic scene, it did rain a little, a "light shower," Daddy called it. I think of him on that afternoon whenever I hear about the rainmakers who traveled across a desperate, scorched America in the Great Depression. Now, reading about the early 1950s, I understand that Daddy was three, maybe four, years into a drought that had taken a toll on our tobacco crops—our income—longer than our family accounts could afford. The word "Depression" is one I associate more with stock markets and ticker tapes. But for a farmer, I realize now, it follows heat and drought.

And then there were the cracks in the ground that break my childhood memories of our farm into a thousand pieces. Ruptures, an inch wide or more, ripped apart our parched lawn, the barnyard, and the fields. I would place my eyeballs at the edge of these dry canyons and stare into the depths wondering if I really could reach China on the other side of the world if I slithered into one. Or was this how Alice fell into her Wonderland? I was skinny in those days, so my sliding into one of these gaping fissures in the earth was not a far-fetched possibility.

Mostly, though, I remember that there was no escape from the heat. Air conditioners had not yet made it to our corner of America, not even into the stores in the nearby small towns like Owenton.

Oscillating electric fans were our only source of relief, though I don't recall that they cooled our houses much. On a mission to whack off my fingers, the menacing fans made as much noise as a World War II bomber squad. Still, when the sun was at high noon and I had no place else to hide, I sprawled in front of their rapid-fire blades and begged for mercy.

The nights were the most difficult. Maybe this was because our daylight hours were expected to be hard and full of work on the farm, but nighttime—oh, that was for rest. If the thermometer were still hanging around ninety at ten o'clock in the evening, however, it would be about 110 in our upstairs bedrooms, and sleep impossible.

In the summer of 1952, when the drought set in, our little house was full of people too hot to sleep. Mother, Daddy, and I lived with Gran Hudson, so that made four. Aunt Sis and her third—maybe fourth—husband were separated, so she arrived early in the summer seeking asylum. About a month later, however, he showed up to woo her back—which he did—and no one had the heart to tell him to leave, since we assumed he was out of work. They both stayed until September. Another relative was having a health crisis, so her two children, about my age, spent the summer with us also. We were a total of eight people, then, in a hot house with three tiny bedrooms.

This was the summer Aunt Sis, notorious for running any good thing into the ground, made pink potato salad for every meal except breakfast. Sometime around the middle of July, deep into the heat and the drought, she accidentally mixed Stanley oven degreaser into the mess instead of Wesson salad oil and nearly sent us all to the hospital. But I digress—the nights are what nearly killed us.

The grown-ups would sit on the porch and fan themselves with folded sheets of the *Lexington Herald* and tell the stories of who had been, of oughts and shoulds and might-have-beens, while we kids smothered a generation of lightning bugs. I'm amazed that the insect didn't land on the endangered species list.

Finally, near midnight, we'd give up and fall into restless beds. One night, Aunt Sis announced that they couldn't take the upstairs bedroom that was as hot as "you know where" any longer.

Later, Daddy would confess he had hoped this meant they were leaving. Instead, Aunt Sis and Husband Number Three or Four carried blankets to the backyard and slept on the ground. Farm people back then didn't believe in camping. Hoboes slept outside— not honest, hardworking people who had perfectly good houses to sleep in. Perhaps keeping up appearances had melted with the heat, however, because Mother relented and let us children sleep outside, too, that night.

The heat wave of 1952 would end, and winter came around again. The drought would end, too, but not until 1955, apparently. Maybe this one will, too. Or maybe it won't, given the way the climate is changing. Hang on, I whisper as I water the ferns, hang on.

CALLA LILY

WHEN YOU ARE RAISED IN A FAMILY that has tilled the same small acreage of earth for generations, you grow up with ghosts. Not haints, not a cold invisible hand or mysterious slamming door. It's the stories of our people that refuse to die. No, that's not quite true. It is we who will not let the stories go, who repeat them, archiving them in our collective memory, like folk ballads or the mythology of the ancients. Never mind that only the details of time and place distinguish our stories from those told by other families around the world. These particular tales belong uniquely to us, and we pass them from grandparent to grandchild, like Aesop's Fables, to teach a moral, to entertain, or to remember who we are.

In the rural Southern landscape of my childhood, these oft-repeated stories helped us survive summer nights, when the humid Kentucky heat brought all movement to a stop and we had only enough energy left to sit in the dark on the porch and listen. They pulled my family through tedious winter days in the tobacco stripping room, when there was only talk to break the monotony of work and to keep us from going stark raving mad. And they led me, a child absorbing their voices, into other people's lives through story, to the realization that "it could have been me."

One of my grandfather's most disturbing tales was about his cousin, Calla Lily Hudson, the pretty girl with the pretty name, who tragically died on her honeymoon. That particular story so haunted me that in adulthood, I felt compelled to research old newspapers and census records to verify what Gran Hudson had told me.

CALLA LILY HUDSON AND BEN DEGARIS were married on September 14, 1910. Her wedding day and mine would be separated by more than half a century and by two world wars. Yet I feel as connected to her as if she passed through here last month. Perhaps that's because the same patch of Owen County land nurtured both of us through infancy and childhood. Her father—my grandfather's Uncle Ed Hudson—once owned the land where my family's farmhouse now stands. Calla Lily was born there during tobacco stripping season in November 1889. Her two siblings would refer to our farm as their "homeplace" until the end of their long lives, and her brother Halcomb requested that his cremated ashes be scattered on the hillside behind our tobacco barn.

Ambitious for greater opportunities for his children, however, Uncle Ed sold his farm in Owen County sometime after the turn of the century and moved his family to the prosperous Bluegrass region. He settled on Leestown Pike, about a mile from the Lexington city limits. In his photos, he looks like a man ready to meet the world straight on, a dapper, handsome man with a merry twinkle in his eye and a confident tilt in his jawline.

By 1910, Uncle Ed's family was thriving in their new location. His son, Halcomb, was enrolled as a student at the University of Kentucky and was on the staff of the Lexington Herald. His two daughters, "educated in the county schools," were described as "popular" in a newspaper social note and were said to have had "many friends in both the county and in town." And the oldest of the daughters, the beautiful Calla Lily, was engaged to marry an upstanding young man from nearby Georgetown, Benjamin DeGaris.

We know more about Calla Lily's death than we do her life. We presume she was intelligent because her two siblings were. We speculate that she had a great sense of humor because her niece and great-nephews do.

But all we really know is that she was as pretty as the flower that shares her name, Calla Lily, the blossom that helps us celebrate weddings and grieves with us at funerals. In the only photo that survives, her blond hair is rolled smoothly into a classic pompadour, framing a face as softly curved as a cherub's. Her white lace camisole, adorned with a locket hanging mid-bodice, has weathered the whims of fashion and is as flattering to her tiny figure now as it was over a century ago. She wears an engagement ring on her left hand, and as her large eyes open wide for the camera, she smiles sweetly, with anticipation, into the future.

Ben and Callie were married in Lexington on a Wednesday. According to newspaper accounts, they traveled that same day to Cincinnati by train, where they spent two nights. On Friday, still on their honeymoon, they returned to Lexington to her parents' home. It would be their last night together.

On Saturday afternoon, Ben DeGaris invited his bride to take a ride in the family's buggy. They returned to her parents' place about six-thirty. As Ben was turning off Leestown Pike into the gate at the home's long driveway, the horse balked. The animal, spooked by the approach of an automobile coming up behind it, backed to the middle of the road.

Ben urged the horse toward the gate again. This time, as the horse neared the gate, it began kicking wildly and again backed into the turnpike. Frightened, Calla Lily jumped out of the buggy toward the middle of the road.

At that star-crossed moment, Mr. Oscar Brown, who was driving "the machine," attempted to slowly pass the stalled horse and buggy. Perhaps he could not easily brake. From the distance of the twenty-first century, however, I scream, "What were you thinking, Mr. Brown?"

The Model T Ford and Callie—both in motion—collided. The blow threw her beneath the wheels, and although Brown tried to stop, all four tires ran over her body. Her chest was crushed.

She would live for about another hour. Long enough to call for doctors. Long enough to give them a little hope. Long enough to watch her bleed to death.

In the newspaper accounts, Uncle Ed "[did] not blame Mr. Brown" and considered "the tragedy entirely accidental." For his part, Brown took to his bed. "His nervous system has received a great shock, it is said, and he is in serious condition."

I THINK ABOUT CALLA LILY whenever I ponder the randomness of tragic news events. And I wonder if this is why my grandfather also was so fixated on her death. Was he searching for meaning where there appears to be none? If he didn't forget her—perhaps if he could remember not to take happiness for granted—could he give purpose to her pointless death? And what of the other lives altered by chance that awful Saturday evening? Did Mr. Brown ever leave his bed and drive "a machine" again? Did Ben DeGaris ever forgive himself for suggesting that nonessential buggy ride? Did Uncle Ed ever regret moving his family to the city, away from the isolated safety of their homeplace in Owen County?

Time has buried those who could answer my questions. From my research I only learned that Ben DeGaris would eventually remarry and live on to the age of ninety. His only child, however, would be named Calla Lily. He lies in the Georgetown Cemetery between his two wives.

And Uncle Ed Hudson? He would die of a self-inflicted gunshot wound in 1925. They brought him back home to Owen County, where he rests with our people.

NAT LEE

DADDY USED TO SAY THAT TINY NATLEE, Kentucky, hunkered on Eagle Creek where two country roads intersect, was the crossroads of the world. Because, he said, you could start from there and go anywhere.

I loved that joke when I was a kid. By then, Natlee was mostly a memory. All that remained of the gristmill that had called it into existence were thick limestone foundation walls near the edge of Eagle Creek. My friend Mable-Dean and I braved thickets of blackberry briars and grass chiggers to scale the mill's ruins. We couldn't have been more excited if we had stumbled upon the lost tomb of Montezuma, and given the denseness of the undergrowth, I wouldn't bet money that he isn't buried in there.

Natlee had also been the site of a post office for scattered stretches in the nineteenth century, but no one I knew could recall getting mail addressed to Natlee. Its single church, Pleasant View Baptist, an historic congregation with tendrils of connections to the storied eighteenth-century Traveling Church, was defunct. Even the building, hand built by Nat Lee himself, had been torn down and the lumber used to build a barn on Orlie Hale's farm. Only an overgrown cemetery edged by a dry-stacked fieldstone wall left any clue that people had ever worshipped together at Natlee.

In the early 1950s, a dramatic, nighttime fire had destroyed the magnificent wooden covered bridge that had once distinguished this crossroads at the creek, and Natlee's last remaining business, a small grocery store, closed a few years later. There were only about four or five houses that could rightly be claimed within the informal city limits of the village. Like us, most folks in the area lived on surrounding farms that might best be described as "near Natlee."

As I grew older, however, I began to understand that Daddy wasn't joking. He was encouraging me, in the way parents will, to believe in myself. About this time, he began to tell me the story of Nat Lee, the founder of Natlee.

Nat Lee, a large man who tipped the scales at near four hundred pounds, also thought big. Born on the Fourth of July in 1825, he married three times and fathered nineteen children. Some say he was kin to General Henry "Light-Horse Harry" Lee. I'm not certain about that, but for sure, one of his grandchildren, Vice Admiral Willis A. Lee Jr. (born at Natlee—another story for another day), became an Olympic gold medalist marksman and a celebrated naval hero of World War II.

Nat, however, gained his fame in a way unique to nineteenth-century rural Kentucky. Down the road from his prosperous gristmill and across the pike from his Natlee house, he set up a modest, wooden distillery not unlike those found in numerous other communities across the state in that era. Working by hand, he then set out to develop the finest sour mash whiskey recipe in America.

He succeeded. In 1893, his whiskey was placed in competition against five thousand other entries at the Chicago World's Fair. His competitors were backed by millions of dollars from companies all over the globe, but Lee's whiskey went to the big show in a local stone jug displayed under a simple signboard that said only, Old fashioned handmade sour mash Kentucky whiskey. It won the gold medal. It was declared the best whiskey on earth—or at least the best that had traveled to the World's Fair.

For the next decade, Lee's whiskey was promoted in advertisements all over America. It was described as "the finest tonic for the old and decrepit" and "ambrosia of the gods, pleasing alike to the sight, taste, and smell, and is recommended by physicians for medicinal purposes." Though production never exceeded fifty-two gallons a day ("not quantity but quality being desired"), the Natlee distillery prospered.

In the early years of the twentieth century, however, the Owen County distillery was destroyed by fire and production never resumed. But by then, Nat Lee had been dead for a good long while and had been laid to rest between his first two wives under a huge stone monument sculpted to look like the trunk of a tree. I don't know what the symbolism of the monument was intended to be. But for me it is a reminder that when you start at the crossroads of the world, you can go anywhere.

HERE ON EAGLE CREEK

ON A STILL DAY, I fancy I hear their ghosts whispering in the thick stand of trees that touches the far horizon. And I remember that Free Station—the four hundred acres owned by the Black men and women emancipated by Susanah Herndon Rogers—lay directly across Eagle Creek from our tobacco fields.

Over the course of 175 years, that land has been sold off in pieces. Today, though it looks much the same as it ever did, what was once called Free Station is only a memory.

Two miles downstream from our farm, beautiful Mountain Island rises up out of Eagle Creek, dividing it. No one lives there now, but it was the center of activity for the area's earliest settlers. The island's fertile land, 110 acres, is still owned by descendants of the African Americans freed by Susanah's brother James Herndon.

Growing up in my family of storytellers, I often heard my grandfather speak of these two free Black enclaves that thrived here on Eagle Creek before the Civil War, and his stories of Free Station and

Mountain Island became a part of "the small acreages of the universe" entrusted to me to remember. I retell them now as I am able—fragmented and filled with conjecture as they must be—the stories of the Herndon siblings, their freed slaves, and the land James and Susanah ("Aunt Sukey," my grandfather always called her) deeded to them.

As I am able—but I cannot know, not viscerally, the whole story of the Black families who lived, worked, and died on those early Eagle Creek settlements before and after their manumission. I am a white child of Kentucky, descended from slave owners, and though I listen, though their descendants and I rode the same bus to school, though we've exchanged what we know of our shared history, I cannot presume to speak from their perspective.

I cannot know the whole story of Susanah and James either, or even if the sister and brother were motivated by the same reasons. They left no diaries or letters for me to peruse. No portraits survive to record a kindly smile or hard mouth. I am left to ponder why they ever thought it right to own other human beings and why they changed their minds. Did they become abolitionist converts, acting from conscience only? Did they hope for atonement? Their reach from the grave to provide financially for those they had once enslaved might suggest that.

Or, finding themselves alone in old age, did they only bargain for the mercy of the Black people who surrounded them? Or perhaps they were contrarians who took delight in disinheriting their scattered relatives?

What follows is only the story as I am able to tell it, stitched together from fragments of public records, the oral history handed down to me, and my imagination. The Herndon siblings and the Black families they freed are woven into the fabric of my rural community's past, but the passage of nearly two centuries has faded the tapestry of all their lives. Still, those who look carefully can see it—the difference they made here on Eagle Creek.

TIME HAS A CRUEL WAY OF TRIVIALIZING HUMAN EXISTENCE, losing the records of our ordinary lives to fire or rot or neglect. Sometimes it ignores our brief stories on earth as though we never existed. I think of the thousands of nameless African American slaves whose descendants seek in vain for recorded traces that they ever lived.

I think, too, of the obscure lives led by many white women during Kentucky's harsh early years, confined by patriarchal restraints, unnoted in the history they lived. They rest in unmarked graves in small country cemeteries, near streams with names like Eagle Creek, where they sleep unnamed, unremembered, until the roll is called up yonder.

The childless Aunt Sukey[1]—Susanah Herndon Rogers—is such a woman, one who left almost no tracks that she ever walked on earth. Her birth and marriage records have not survived courthouse fires and floods. Her name is not found in her father's will or in a husband's will or on a tombstone. She died before census records included the names of household members. The source of her property is a mystery. Knowledge of her lingers only because she dared to speak the names of others who could not speak for themselves.

---

1. I have found no kinship between my grandfather, George Hudson, and Susanah Herndon Rogers, yet he always referred to her as Aunt Sukey, as did his cousin Vernon Hudson, who lived in view of her gravesite. The title may have been a custom of time and place. However, I believe that within the large Silas Hudson clan, she may have been referred to as Aunt Sukey because Silas Hudson's first wife, Polina Abbott, was a sister to John and Ann Herndon Ficklin's daughter-in-law. Polina's mother was also a Herndon and could have been related, though I do not know how.

Like the ringing of a bell, the names of seventeen slaves, emancipated in her 1838 will, echo through history: Ailcey, Garrett, Theophilus, Christiann, Merrit, Rose, Charles, Andrew, Warren, Harry, Marriann, William, Gabrial, Hillery, Liddy, Tildy… In naming them, in freeing them, she left a trace that she, too, had passed this way. Yet that will is signed only with her mark. She could not write her own name.

Occasionally, an individual slave had been given freedom, but never before had so many been freed in Owen County at one time. In her repentance, Aunt Sukey went further. She gave her large plantation of 403 acres to her emancipated slaves outright, with the advice they sell it and set sail for equality and happiness in the African colony of Liberia where they could be "truly free."

I can find no record that any of Aunt Sukey's former slaves took her advice. Instead, they remained for several generations on the land she had given them, each family on its own individual farm, and their agrarian community became known as Free Station. From what I can determine from oral and recorded history, they mostly were left alone by their white neighbors, in an era and place that respected land ownership.

Over time, however, as descendants multiplied exponentially and the younger generations drifted to nearby cities, the families began to sell off their inheritance from Aunt Sukey. By the late 1940s when my grandfather purchased 250-plus acres of what had once been Free Station, it already had passed through several non-heir owners. Only Eagle Creek separated his newly purchased acreage from his other land, our homeplace, and so we always referred to our portion of what had once nobly been called Free Station as simply "the farm across the creek."

Yet my grandfather George Hudson's stories about Aunt Sukey and the Black people who came before us on the land stayed with me. Born in 1878, he had known many of the Black heirs and talked about Aunt Sukey's having given them her land as though she had just walked out the door last month. I became intrigued with her, a woman with progressive ideas out of sync with most of her neighbors in a time when women were not expected—or allowed—to have ideas of their own. What had edged her to the right side of history, a female born in the eighteenth century into a slaveholding family in Virginia, unable to read, isolated in adulthood in a rural, Kentucky community that would side with the Confederate States of America within two decades?

Her story remains a puzzle with missing pieces. However, over the years, I have learned enough to reconstruct her plausible journey toward the intersection of conscience and compassion.

Although no one knows when Susanah Herndon Rogers was born, her will confirms what my grandfather told me. She was a sister to James Herndon, one of the earliest settlers on Eagle Creek. Unlike his sister, James left clear tracks in Kentucky records as a public official, businessman, and landowner. Today, however, he is only remembered by local people as the man who freed his twenty-two slaves in the 1850s and gave them Mountain Island. Susanah, however, decided to free her slaves twelve or more years before James did and left them four times as much land.

It is not clear who their parents were. I've long thought, as historian Dr. James Bryant did, that she and James were the children of Lewis Herndon, whose Scott County will is dated 1789 and was probated in 1798. Lewis's will appointed his son, James, coexecutor of his estate. However, the document does not mention Susanah's name. It does include unidentified "other living children" among the heirs, but there is no mention of Susanah specifically.

A number of circumstantial clues, however, persuade me that Lewis Herndon is the father of Susanah and James. The most significant is the repetition of Lewis's mother's unusual name, Valentine, among the enslaved families on James Herndon's Mountain Island. Also, Lewis Herndon's family history was connected to a plantation named Locust Grove in Spotsylvania County, Virginia—and each of Susanah's freed heirs took the last name Locust.

If Susanah and James were Lewis Herndon's children, as I believe, then fate brought them face to face with the Rev. John H. Ficklin who, according to his marriage bond, married Lewis Herndon's daughter, Ann/Anna. Ficklin, a Baptist preacher, is said to have been one of Kentucky's most outspoken opponents of slavery. He likely influenced Aunt Sukey and set her conscience on fire or at least brought it to a slow simmer.

Then, as now, the church did not speak with one voice on the social issues of the day. Many, perhaps most, Kentucky Christians were strong supporters of slavery, including the powerful Baptist leader, the Rev. Elijah Craig, who owned large numbers of slaves. Yet some of the loudest abolitionist voices sounded in nineteenth-century Kentucky came from the pulpit of Baptist preachers like John Ficklin.

Aunt Sukey would have had difficulty avoiding Ficklin, even if he were not married to her sister Ann. He had numerous connections to her narrow world, especially to the Stamping Ground farm community in Scott County, where her parents had settled in the late eighteenth century. Described as a "fiery" speaker, a man such as Ficklin could have preached Aunt Sukey's soul to the edge of Hell. Then he may have held out salvation for her and whispered the name of the Promised Land—Liberia.

While Liberia did not become an independent country until July 26, 1847, the American Colonization Society (ACS) had established an expatriate colony for emancipated slaves on the western coast of Africa as early as 1821. Kentucky Senator Henry Clay was among its most ardent and prominent supporters. Indeed, by 1828, the Kentucky chapter of the ACS had purchased forty acres in what is now Liberia and established the state of "Kentucky in Africa," which included a settlement named "Clay-Ashland."

The notion of returning Black slaves to Africa after their families had been in America for two or three hundred years strikes most people today as bizarre and cruel. Even then, abolitionists divided along the lines of "assimilation" here or "recolonization" there. However, for many, Liberia was seen as a compassionate answer to the "race problem," since many of even the most fervent opponents of slavery at that time did not think free people of color would ever be able to enjoy full equality in America. That sentiment is echoed in the language of Aunt Sukey's will: "I recommend them to emigrate to Liberia...where they will not only be free but be entitled to privileges of free citizens...."

It is significant, I think, that Susanah's brother-in-law Ficklin had been a protégé of US Senator Richard Mentor Johnson of Great Crossing in Scott County (who later would become Van Buren's vice president). Johnson, in turn, was a very close friend of Henry Clay. Thus, Ficklin, making the moral argument for emancipation in the pulpits of Kentucky's rural Baptist churches, would have been well-informed about Henry Clay's vision of Liberia. Ficklin himself had probably met Clay through Johnson and had likely heard Clay speak publicly on the subject. Described as a man of "strong intellect," he also would have read in the newspapers of the day about the ongoing conversation surrounding the American Colonization

Society and Liberia. Aunt Sukey herself may have had an opportunity to hear Clay speak in her native Stamping Ground or in adjacent Great Crossing at some point in her life.

And so I am reminded that then, as now, it was difficult to be unaware of the major ideas circulating in American culture. Aunt Sukey, illiterate but likely as intelligent as her brother James Herndon, may have been isolated, but she would not have been insulated from conversations surrounding the most complex issue of the century.

IT'S UNCLEAR WHOM AUNT SUKEY MARRIED. The probate of her Owen County will identifies her as the widow of William Rogers. However, I can find no marriage record for her to Rogers or to anyone else, although by the 1830 census, a "Susanah Rogers" was a widowed "head of household" in neighboring Scott County. Nor can I find her mentioned in the will of anyone named William Rogers. Adding confusion, the large Scott County Rogers family repeated the name William within parallel generations, ascending and descending. And if Aunt Sukey had biological children, I have found no mention of them. Other than her emancipated slaves, the only heir mentioned in her will is her brother James, who was given her coin silver spoons.

Susanah's will was written in 1838, but she would live for another nine years. From the distance of the twenty-first century, I find myself quarreling with Aunt Sukey for not freeing her slaves sooner. How did she justify to God her continued use of them until her death?

I can understand that she needed her land to provide for herself. However, having seized upon the idea of Liberia as the most viable way toward true freedom for her slaves, she could have rationalized that she had to give them her plantation—the wherewithal to reach Africa—once she freed them. It should not be ignored that she moved from Scott County to nearby Owen County in 1837 with her mind already set on writing her will and finding a way to help these enslaved individuals find freedom in Liberia.

With the 1835 settlement of a famous land dispute involving over forty thousand acres in Owen, Scott, and Harrison counties (portions of that case reached the United States Supreme Court), the Widow Rogers saw an opportunity to buy 403 acres of Owen County land near the property of her brother James. From her will, it appears that James bought the land on her behalf in exchange for five slaves. This transaction seems odd, given her intention to free all her slaves, but I assume she had no other means to purchase land. Perhaps she even elicited a promise from James to free these five at *his* death, which he did.

What we do know is that in 1837, she transferred all her slaves from Scott County to her new Owen County plantation. By October 1838, the will was written that would free those slaves at her death and make it possible for them to either emigrate to Liberia or to remain on the land divided equally among them.

The New Columbus/Natlee community adjacent to Free Station was not free of the South's prevailing racial prejudice in the decades after the Civil War. While Kentucky did not officially secede from the Union, Owen County sent a higher percentage of its eligible men to fight for the Confederacy than any other Kentucky county. However, I have found no evidence of Ku Klux Klan (KKK) activity in the community surrounding Free Station, even though the virulent KKK wreaked havoc in other sections of Owen. I am left to wonder if Aunt Sukey's early manumission of her slaves in the 1840s—and the subsequent respect that the landowning citizens of Free Station garnered locally—were the antidote to violence, an antidote that other parts of the county did not have.

Today only one small parcel of Free Station remains in the possession of the former slaves' descendants. In my childhood, a tiny, gentle man known as "Shorty" Vinegar lived alone in a small house on that twenty or so acres. Now his land is unoccupied, a place where his great-nephews, who live in the city, come to ride horses and camp. It's surrounded by the acreage my grandfather purchased in the 1940s and is landlocked—the owners must cross our farm to reach theirs, as we in turn must cross theirs to reach sections of ours. We have lived in harmony as neighbors, each on our respective piece of Aunt Sukey's plantation, for over seventy years.

A mile or so from our place, Aunt Sukey is buried beside her brother James between two ancient cedar trees on the mainland across from Mountain Island. I'm told that a large fieldstone once marked her gravesite, but if so, time has removed it. The only other graves in the country cemetery are those of the Black men and women who shared the siblings' lives and a few descendants of those Black families.

These graves, too, are unmarked except in legend. I hope—I pray— Aunt Sukey's soul rests with them in peace.

★

IN FEBRUARY OF 1850, JAMES HERNDON, lifelong bachelor, woke up one morning, his arthritis worse than usual, his energy and ambition gone, and realized that he was an old man. He also was the second-largest slave owner in Owen County, Kentucky. He hadn't set out to become that. More than most of that time, he'd been exposed to abolitionist thinking. His sister, Susanah, had emancipated her slaves some years earlier, and their brother-in-law, the Rev. John Herndon Ficklin, had stood in the pulpit as a fiery critic of slavery.

It's unclear exactly when Herndon arrived in the Kentucky territory. It's likely that he walked in with other family members on the Wilderness Trail in the early 1780s with the Traveling Church of Spotsylvania County, Virginia. But by the late 1790s, he had wandered north of the Kentucky River, where he happened upon Eagle Creek, a tributary nearly ninety miles long that eventually empties into the Kentucky only a few miles before it merges with the mighty Ohio.

To Herndon's delight, he not only found rich bottomland along the creek, but also a 110-acre island formed at a point where the creek forked into two branches before converging again further downstream. Mountain Island, higher than the surrounding valley, was a natural fort, and it had fresh springs and fertile soil.

He settled in and prospered. In 1812, he erected a mill on the island that became the center of the sparsely populated region. In 1817, he was licensed to open a tavern there, too. Literate and capable, he was appointed to numerous official positions in the new land, ranging from justice of the peace to high sheriff. He acquired more slaves. By the 1820 census, he owned thirteen. As his responsibilities increased, he could ignore any quiet voice within his heart and could justify to himself the ownership of the men and women he needed to cultivate his fields and tame the frontier.

Oddly, his name is absent from the carefully kept records of the Mountain Island Baptist Church, which stood almost in sight of his log house. Both his home and the church were built on the mainland bank of Eagle Creek, overlooking Mountain Island. The church was established in 1801 by members of his parents' old Traveling Church from Virginia, led into the wilderness by the Craig brothers, who would become famous in Central Kentucky history. For many years, Mountain Island Baptist was the only church in the community and was an important social and political force, so his absence seems notable. But it's possible to imagine that Herndon stood apart from the church because he was uneasy in the presence of God—or in the presence of Christians who insisted slavery was God's will.

Certainly he was a man of contradictions. As part of the WPA Federal Writers Project in the 1930s, John Forsee interviewed the descendants of Herndon's former slaves. They told Forsee that Herndon sometimes gave his slaves a colt or calf to raise as their own and to barter. From time to time, he also permitted them to work for other neighbors by the day and keep the money they earned. He allowed one Black man, Valentine, to work two years for a neighbor, Dick Sparrow, so that "Tiney" could purchase his wife from Sparrow with his labor. Valentine's wife was a free woman forever after, purchased by her husband's love, and in a peculiar way, with Herndon's assistance.

Yet Herndon claimed ownership of the children born to Valentine and his free wife. And though it cannot be documented, some descendants of the Mountain Island families believe that Herndon fathered at least one child by a female slave. Dolly Vinegar, who inherited a life interest in Herndon's log house and who was given a larger portion of land than the other heirs in his will, is definitely listed as a "mulatto" in the 1860 census. This terminology in that era would indicate that she had a white father.

Furthermore, according to Forsee, Herndon promised Dolly that he would never sell her children or any of the Mountain Island people. This promise was supposedly made when a slave trader once came to the island seeking to purchase Dolly's son "Big George"—a giant who stood over seven feet tall and who would later travel with the Barnum & Bailey Circus.

BY 1850, HERNDON WAS EIGHTY-FOUR YEARS OLD and owned twenty-two slaves. His sister, Susanah, had been dead for three years. It's easy to imagine that his slaves had become restless as they worked alongside Aunt Sukey's freed slaves, and he was fearful of insurrection. Perhaps (as Forsee wrote) he had promised Dolly, years earlier, when he dismissed the slave trader, that he would free them all at his death. Perhaps with eternity looming, he got religion. After all, if the thief on the cross could be forgiven, surely God could still be persuaded to deal gently with James Herndon. For whatever reason, Herndon decided to free all of his slaves while he still lived.

He had the legal papers drawn up, and he presented them in county court on February 19, 1850. He assumed this would be a simple process, as it had been so in the past, when his sister Susanah freed her slaves. The divisive political winds, however, that would culminate in the Civil War a decade later were already blowing in Owen County. (By early 1860, the Kentucky legislature would enact a bill prohibiting the emancipation of any slaves unless they immediately left the state, and free Black individuals who entered Kentucky were to be jailed.) The judge refused to admit Herndon's emancipation document on a technicality—the slaves were not present in the courtroom. The judge continued the case until the court convened in April.

On April 15, 1850, Herndon was back in fiscal court with all of the slaves, but again the judge refused to hear him. This time, the judge ruled that Herndon would have to produce a $21,000 bond to ensure that the freed men and women would not become a "burden… to the Commonwealth."

Herndon was stunned. He could not—or would not—come up with the unprecedented amount of the bond. He filed a bill of exception and then left, but he vowed to return. The remaining three years of his life were devoted to one legal battle after another in an attempt to free his slaves. He did not succeed.

In death, he tried again. His will not only emancipated his enslaved men, women, and children, but it also deeded Mountain Island to them and their heirs forever.[2] After additional legal skirmishes and a change in the sitting judge, the court finally honored Herndon's wishes in August 1853, after several of Herndon's neighbors—Silas Hudson, Richard Sparrow, and L.D. Bassett—posted security bonds as required by Kentucky law to free a slave.

Today, over 150 years later, descendants of Joshua Sr., Dolly, Richard, Valentine, Joshua Jr., Jerry, Willis, Fanny, George, Milley, Susana, William, John, Wiat, Mary, James Lewis, Ann Marie, Annet Jane, George Warren, Charles William, Dolly Carroll, and Masiat still own Mountain Island.

---

2. Kentucky law now limits to one generation the length of time land can be held in trust without the heirs regaining the right to sell. Although at the time of this writing (2021) Mountain Island was still owned by the descendants of Herndon's island slaves, it was no longer held in the original trust established by James Herndon's will.

POLINA'S GRAVE

WE SCRAMBLED OVER AN ANCIENT STONE WALL, the Kentucky kind, built with limestone gathered from the hayfields, stacked and held together only with sweat. The first thing I saw in this abandoned place was the giant cross, one rugged tree felled by an old wind, come to rest without design at a perfect right angle across the midsection of another. The old conundrum flitted through my mind: If a tree falls in a forest and no one hears it, does it make a sound? Can the dead hear?

The dry, dusty smell of early October mingled with the odor of our perspiration. It had been a long, warm walk up the hill to this forgotten, walled garden. The grave markers in the little country cemetery were hidden by tall wildflowers covered with delicate white blooms undisturbed by scythe or cow.

"Wildflowers?" Ernie said when I remarked on their beauty. "No, these weeds are white snakeroot. If a cow eats them, the milk will poison whoever drinks it. They think that's what killed Abraham Lincoln's mother."

"Really?" I was stunned into silence. How could plants that pretty be so lethal? And how ironic that they flourished here among the dead, that they were protected by the stone wall built to keep intruders out.

We'd come to explore this old country graveyard that rests on top of a hill not far from our farm in Owen County. It's called the Sebree Cemetery in recent historical inventories because the Sebree family heirs owned the surrounding farmland for decades. The only marked graves, however, connect to a man named Joseph Abbott, unrelated to the Sebree family, as far as I can determine, and unrelated to me.

Joseph Abbott did, however, own many acres of land on Eagle Creek in the early nineteenth century, and thus he figures prominently into the early history of this rural community. It was Joseph Abbott's descendants who'd come the year before, traveled from Atlanta, they said, to pull the old stones out of the earth and reclaim the cemetery's dignity.

THEY'D CLEANED THE STONES AS BEST THEY COULD and righted those that were leaning. Some, separated by time and nature from their original sites, they'd propped against scattered trees, orphaned, alone.

It was one of those orphaned stones that had lured me here. *We dug a thin, smooth rock out of the ground, covered by several feet of mud,* my correspondent wrote. *It was scribed as follows: Polina Hudson Died (illegible day and month) 1850. Note: Both N's were carved backwards.*

For decades, genealogists thought Polina Abbott Hudson was buried in an unmarked grave, but now these men from Georgia claimed to have found her headstone. I wanted to see it for myself.

I wanted to see it on behalf of my mother, too, who had been fascinated by Polina's poignant story and had repeated it to me many times. For reasons difficult to explain to those who do not ponder such things, it bothered Mother that poor Polina was buried in an unmarked grave.

Polina was Joseph Abbott's daughter and my great-great-grand-father Silas Hudson's first wife. Described by her contemporaries as "a good Christian woman," she supposedly persuaded her husband, Silas, "who liked to drink too much," to right the course of his life. Under her influence, he went on to become a well-known minister and lawyer in the area. He lived into his eighties, respected—even revered—and is buried in the Methodists' well-kept cemetery beneath a towering, elaborate stone.

Polina, however, died at age thirty. She left behind eight children, including a newborn son who survived her by only a few months. Just weeks after the baby's death, Polina's fifteen-month-old, Helena, toppled from her highchair and burned to death in the open fireplace. Helena's tragic fate was repeated to every generation of Hudson children for the next century, a warning to be careful—oh so careful— when we got near the fireplace or the big coal-burning stove. To fully appreciate Polina's tragic fate, however, we children had to become adults ourselves, perhaps even mothers ourselves.

But Polina's husband, Silas, gets our sympathy, too. I can only imagine the despair that swamped him in 1850 as he lost his wife, Polina, and then, in quick succession, their two youngest children. Perhaps it was desperation, rather than love, that pushed him to remarry in late 1851. His second wife, *my* double-great-grandmother, would raise Polina's surviving children and bear Silas eight more.

WE WADED THROUGH THE KNEE-HIGH FLOWERS looking for whomever we could find, but with an eye out for Polina. We found the newest graves first, the ones dating to the 1880s. Those markers were marble, ornately carved by a stonecutter in prosperous times. The oldest graves dated to the early 1840s. These were marked by field-stones from the surrounding hills, names and dates crudely gouged out by a knife.

"Here it is," Ernie said when we'd nearly given up. Leaning against a hackberry tree on the far side of the graveyard, Polina's headstone was concealed by the tall, flowering snakeroot. I bent to feel the smooth, ancient rock with my hands, my finger tracing the faint letters of her name, POLINA HUDSON. My touch lingered on the two backward Ns and then on the date, 1850. Who had dug these letters and numbers into a fieldstone so long ago? Her grieving husband Silas? One of her children?

HUNDREDS, MAYBE THOUSANDS, of these family cemeteries dot Kentucky's rural countryside. Some have succumbed to creeping vegetation, livestock, or vandals. But most endure, with occasional help from a distant relative or a kind neighbor. Why? Why do they endure? Why does some odd soul in each succeeding generation step forward to whack away at the bushes, to pull the fallen stones from the ground? I'm not sure. We're a curious lot, those of us who love and respect old cemeteries.

Perhaps we've glimpsed how brief our time here on earth will be, and so we come to affirm both the importance of individual life and the flow of all life through the generations. Or perhaps we come to weep for the art—the effort—the names and dates hand-chiseled into fieldstones, even as crops called for tending and babies cried to eat.

The giant cross, formed by fallen trees, lay in a patch of sunlight as the sun eased lower in the west. It was time for us to go. I traced the backward Ns with my finger one more time. It is Polina Abbott Hudson's land, inherited from her father, Joseph Abbott, that I call home, the farm where I grew up, that I still own. "Thank you," I whispered, in case the dead aren't deaf.

DEATH OF A FARMER

JANUARY IS A MUDDY MONTH HERE. The mud pulls at our ankles and even our knees, as though it would take us with it on its long slide to the spring floods. Or maybe it's trying to hang on to us, wanting to stay put. I don't know. But more years than not, the snow forms to the north and wears itself out pushing south across the Ohio River. By the time it reaches Kentucky, it's a thin, relentless rain that beats our old hillsides into giving up. So, when I remember the day it happened, all I remember is the rain. As if our tears were not sufficient for our emotions, it rained and rained and rained, until the broad, low bottoms that lie along Eagle Creek were flooded.

The rain finally stopped after five days, but by then, Daddy had turned the tractor over on the slick hill behind the barn and crushed the life right out of his bones. By then, we had sung the hymns and eaten the neighbor-brought casseroles and, of course, we had buried him but not until the hearse sank its wheels deep into the graveyard mud and had to be pushed and pulled to higher ground.

When the rain stopped, nothing would do Mother but to walk out there on the ridge, through all that mud and misty wind, and her with her bad hip, and climb down that hillside so she could see, so she could know. Oh Lord, we were a mess. The mud could have taken us under, dragged us clear to the bottoms, and buried our bodies along with our souls, right then and there, and I don't guess anyone could have found a trace of us—at least not until the creek returned to its banks.

I was just so mad at everything, at Mother, at Daddy, even at this old hilly land itself—this land that we had loved and taken care of and called our own since the beginning of time. My eyes ached from crying.

"Stop it," Mother said. "Stop crying!"

I knew that I had to do what she said.

THAT'S WHERE WE WERE WHEN CHARLIE FOUND US. Charlie lives on the farm that joins ours, and he's raised Mother and Daddy's tobacco ever since he was old enough. I've known him all of my life.

"What are you two doing out here?" His voice scolded us. His voice loved us.

I turned Mother over to him, glad for his strength. Slowly, carefully, I followed them back up the hill to the barn where some of the tobacco was still hanging, waiting to be stripped and sold. The rain had brought the dried tobacco "in case," as the men said, made it damp and supple, easy to handle, ready for Charlie to strip the leaves from the stalks. That is why he had come, to check on the tobacco, he said.

When we finally got to the barn, I was oddly grateful for the familiar odor of the dried crop. It overwhelmed my senses, shutting out everything else but the cold dampness of the barn. It hung like dust in my nostrils—an old smell, strong, irritating, but sustaining. Oh Daddy, where are you, I almost cried out, but Charlie was there, so I only hugged myself and stomped my feet for warmth.

In spite of myself, I found myself looking out the open barn door we had just entered, toward the old walnut tree that stands beyond the barn. My grandfather and I used to sit there when I was little, on a big rock that's halfway buried in the ground, and crack walnuts. I remembered exactly how the farm had looked to me then. We would sit there together and look out over the hillside into the broad Eagle Creek bottoms that seemed to stretch out below as far as I could see. I remembered wanting to walk and walk until I reached Eagle Creek and its row of white, bony sycamore trees that reached from one far side of the bottom on the left to the other far side on the right. I wanted to walk from where I was, from under the walnut tree on top of the world, to the other side of the world, where the sky met the earth. And we would sit there, Gran and I, and he would tell me the stories about the old people who had come before us on this land, even the Indians, who had left only their arrowheads in our tobacco fields to tell their tales.

Gran had died long ago, when I was only a child, but on this day, I could remember him as though he had walked out the door last week like my father had. Suddenly, I realized that Daddy must have run the tractor wheels over the big rock by the walnut tree before the tractor veered down the hill toward the bottoms.

When we were rested, we went on, our steps slow and heavy through the barnyard ruts, and from there into Mother's pretty yard, all gone to mush now, and past the rose garden, mounded and wrapped for the winter. Finally, we reached the steps to the screened porch. We pulled off our muddiness there and sought the warmth of the kitchen. Numbly, we pretended to eat ham sandwiches, but mostly we drank the hot, creamy coffee and picked at the caramel icing on a near-gone jam cake that careened on the cake stand. We remarked again at the kindness of those who had brought in so much food, knowing that we could not cope, knowing that we would not eat without their help.

They had, in fact, carried us from the moment of Mother's first cry for help. They had appeared instantly from all directions and held us in their arms and made the calls and put us to bed.

The men had sat silently on the hillside for hours by Daddy's broken body, waiting first for the EMTs, then the coroner, then the machines, big enough, strong enough, to pull his body out from under the muddy hill. When we tried to thank them, their eyes looked away.

"It might have been me," first one man said and then another. "Could have been..."

Before the awful night was over, a hundred or more must have come, from every corner of our lives. The men went out into the night, to the barn, then to the hill, trying to follow the tracks, trying to understand. The women crushed quietly into the house and made coffee and sandwiches.

"It might have been mine," first one woman said and then another. "Could have been..."

Now the house was empty. Even Charlie had returned to the barn. Mother and I sat on at the table alone, saying nothing, but aware of the television playing in the empty room next to us. War was exploding in the Middle East. Yes, we knew that, but what was there to say about it? Armageddon filled my heart, and I was annoyed with the poet for being wrong. The world does too end with a bang. I would have preferred a whimper.

Finally, we began the ritual we had hit upon in our grief. We found a strange comfort in the endless reexamination of the horror.

Mother said again, "He was so happy that morning, kidding and cutting up just like he always did. The last thing I said to him was, 'I'll be back in time to watch the UK basketball game with you on TV.' And then I drove to the beauty shop. Who would think he'd be dead when I got home?"

I asked again, "Do you think he knew what was happening? Could he have had a small stroke? Why was he on that hill?"

And Mother said, as she always did, "Yes, he must have had a little stroke. He must have been disoriented. Because there was no reason in the world for him to be on that hill with the tractor."

And then we would retrace the path the tractor must have taken from the far barn, going slowly toward the near barn, then veering irrationally around the walnut tree, away from the barns on the ridge, and driving in a straight line down the hill toward the bottoms. Could he have looked away at a calf, perhaps, and looking up saw that he was headed toward the tree? In his surprise, could he have steered right, toward the hillside, instead of left, toward the lane, and then gone into an irreversible slide? No, no, surely he had not made such a mistake. Surely he was disoriented from a little stroke, surely disorientation had caused him to turn right instead of left.

We had done this about a thousand times by now, but in the retelling, we sometimes happened upon a different nuance, a fresh speculation.

"Do you think he suffered much?" this from me, again and again.

"Oh, no. It had to be quick. It's obvious he was steering that tractor until it turned over. I know your Daddy. When the tractor started to slide, he would have been confident he could steer it to the bottoms. And when it turned over, well, it would have been quick. He couldn't have suffered. No," this answer from Mother, over and over.

Finally, from me, "What are we going to do with the farm now?"

Silence from Mother, and then, "Our roots are buried here. I was born here, your grandfather, his grandfather—"

"But Mother, how are we going to manage the farm, the cattle and hay, the tobacco?"

"I'm going to ask Charlie to carry on. If he will," Mother answered.

"We're not selling?"

"No," Mother replied. There was finality in her voice.

Slowly, Mother walked to the kitchen sink with its window that looks out over the hillside and the bottoms. When she spoke again, there was a tone in her voice that I had not heard before.

"Did I ever tell you that my cousin Halcomb was cremated? Uncle Ed Hudson's son? He was the only person I ever knew to be cremated. They brought his ashes back here, scattered them on the hill. That was the year after the old house burned. I made an angel food cake for them."

She leaned in closer to the window and stared into the January grayness. "I wonder if your daddy ran into Halcomb when he died?"

NATLEE 2020

I SAVED THE HOUSE, MOTHER, though I couldn't save much inside the house. Daddy's fine felt hats, the ones you had left in the closet, were eaten up by moths. I know why you kept them. You said seeing them hanging there kept him alive for you, like he'd only stepped out on the farm and would be back in an hour. You said that I wouldn't understand. I did understand. But the dust and the moth holes—I couldn't save them any longer.

I saved the house, its bones, all the old wooden doors with their vintage doorknobs, and all the original light fixtures. I even left Daddy's UK Wildcats calendars on the back of his closet door, at your granddaughter's request. But I couldn't save the battered storm door on the front. I think you'd like the new security screen door that replaced it.

I saved the house's kitchen cabinets and the magazine recipes you had taped to the back of the cabinet doors. (I'm going to make those oatmeal bar cookies, the ones you baked in a Pyrex dish.) But I didn't save the mismatched dishes that you left behind in the kitchen for your occasional visits to the farmhouse. Your leaving them was a good idea twenty-nine years ago, when you moved to the apartment after Daddy died. But it's been thirteen years now since you yourself passed on, and I can't put off any longer this last bit of cleaning out. We'll use paper and plastic when we picnic there.

I did save an ornate lid from a missing soup tureen. I have no memory of it so I'm guessing it was a treasure Daddy picked up at an estate sale, as he liked to do. I propped it in the living room bookcase beside Daddy's books. I think it looks pretty there. Oh, I did have to throw away a lot of his books that mildew and critters had damaged. Fortunately, though, the bugs didn't seem to relish munching on his beloved collection of Harvard classics. I cleaned them up and they strut on as proudly as ever on your built-in bookshelves.

I didn't keep your Kroger giveaway plates with the gray and pink flowers. You once had a whole matching set, and they were your "good" dishes until Daddy bought you the Lenox china. But you never much liked them because you didn't like pink. And everybody had some. I did admire some knockoff Spode plates I found. I think Uncle Murf gave them to you for Christmas one year. But only three have survived, and I reminded myself that I have too much dishware as it is. Some of your coffee mugs were 1960s Ashland Oil freebies with a fill-up. Those brought back sweet memories of Ernie's early working years with that company, but I let them go.

I saved the house, but your custom-made avocado green draperies had dry-rotted. I dumped them into three of those big, black plastic garbage bags. After forty years, I think we got our money's worth out of them, but I felt guilty tossing them. I remember how proud you were of them and what good care you took of your things.

But I saved the house, Mother. I had a professional paint the outside, and the kids are helping me paint the inside. I've cleaned it crevice to crevice because I know how you hated dirt, that cleanliness is next to godliness—but gee, bugs can find a lot of cracks to hide in and die at an old place.

I saved the view of the valley from the house, too, because that's why the house is there on the hill. The pastures are mowed, the barn painted, the fences mended. And we built a deck off the back porch, where we can sit and look out over the valley.

I'm saving the stories, too, but it's hard to get them to listen. I've told them how your father put the view together piece by piece, twenty or fifty acres at a time, as he had the money, as it came up for sale. How it took him a quarter of a century to do that, starting as a young man in 1908. How he hung on to it through the Great Depression that hit in 1929, when others were giving up and cattle and tobacco sold for less than it took to raise them.

And when everything closed down during the COVID-19 pandemic, I told the grandchildren about Roosevelt's "bank holiday." How the banks closed shut in 1933 like the mall had done in 2020 and how my grandfather went to a man who had some cash money, how he talked for an entire day to convince the man to lend him that cash money so he could go to the courthouse steps and buy the last half of our valley view, the one that the federal land bank had repossessed from a long-gone neighbor. I told them how that was the proudest accomplishment of my grandfather's life, how he had convinced the man to lend him that cash money at the bottom of the Great Depression on the strength of his word. "Character collateral," he called it.

I told them about our people, the Hudsons, who settled on this piece of earth in the 1840s, sturdy folk, survivors, and how some of us have been here on this piece of bottomland ever since. Then I told them to look beyond our wide valley to the yon side of Eagle Creek, where a great forest stands. That's ours, too, I told them, but it wasn't always.

And so I told them about Aunt Sukey, how in the beginning the land across the creek was hers, and how she shocked her small world by freeing her seventeen slaves a good long while before the Civil War and gave them all her land outright, and how it became known as Free Station. I told them that over there the ancient boundaries of the land are still marked by dry-stacked stone walls built by those Black hands. I told them how it was sold off, piece by piece, over a century and how my grandfather bought a big chunk of Aunt Sukey's old place in 1947 when it came up for sale, because he could, and because he could see it from here on the high hill, where the house sits, as he looked out across the bottoms, across Eagle Creek, to where the sky meets the earth.

I SAVED THE BONES—the house, the view, the stories. It was quite a bit, but it wasn't much. I couldn't even save Daddy's hats, Mother.

But this is what I did when the COVID-19 pandemic closed down America, when political hysterics wafted up from Washington like indecipherable smoke signals rising to the clouds, and I was afraid I might lose my mind in the awful newness of these times. I saved what I could, of who we were, of who I am, for the children, I said, and maybe so, but mostly for me, to hear your voice again and Daddy's, too, wise, steady, laughing, guiding me through a maze that none of us have traveled before.

"That all of us have traveled before," I hear you whisper in reply.

There is nothing new under the sun, the preacher said.

And so I saved the house. I saved what I could, perhaps even me.

I hope that is enough, Mother, because I couldn't save Daddy's hats.

ACKNOWLEDGMENTS

SMALL ACREAGES WOULD NOT HAVE COME INTO BEING without the host of average angels who surround me. Some of them are no longer living—many friends of the journey, my parents, grandparents, aunts, uncles—but their voices live on within me and help me tell their stories. Other angels are very much alive, however, and I am profoundly grateful for their here and now support.

I especially want to thank Virginia Underwood of Shadelandhouse Modern Press for accepting Small Acreages for publication even as she and I and the entire world struggle to survive a hundred-year pandemic. Her vision of what the book could become, her confidence in it, and her guidance have turned it into reality.

I borrowed the great Wendell Berry's eloquent language to title Small Acreages and to name three of its five sections. I wish to thank him for giving me permission to do this. I also am forever grateful to have found my people in his beautiful books, and I do so thank him for giving voice—and bestowing such dignity—to our Kentucky culture.

I also am indebted to my longtime writing mentor, Leatha Kendrick, not only for her editing advice as I separated the wheat from the chaff in the early stages of this project, but also for her assurance that the world really did need one more book—my book. Without her encouragement, I am unsure I would have continued wrestling these stubborn, separate essays into a whole.

Sherry Chandler and Ami Piccirilli—my long-time friends and gifted "trusted readers"—cannot be thanked enough for reading early drafts of these essays over the years that they were written. I am forever thankful for their honesty in telling me when I got it right and (especially) when I didn't.

Gratitude is also due the *Kentucky Humanities* Council (KHC), its Executive Director Henry William Goodman, and Marianne Stoess, editor of Kentucky Humanities magazine, for helping me share my Kentucky stories over the past decade. Small Acreages emerged as I wrote for the back page of the magazine and spoke on behalf of KHC to audiences across the state about the importance of preserving our personal and local stories.

I also wish to thank *The Owenton News-Herald*, which has published my column Georgia: On My Mind since 2004, and its kind editors over the years, most recently Molly Haines. Many of the essays in *Small Acreages* emerged from ideas first tentatively explored in the column.

And to my husband Ernie—my one-man technical team, research assistant, photographer, and constant cheerleader—thank you for over a half century of love and support.

ATTRIBUTIONS

"Natlee 2020" was written in response to Margaret Renkl's essay "What I Saved," which is included in her book *Late Migrations*. Minneapolis: Milkweed Editions, 2019.

"Our Quilts" was written for Linda Elisabeth LaPinta's forthcoming book. *Kentucky Quilts and Quiltmakers: Three Centuries of Creativity, Community, and Commerce*. Lexington: University Press of Kentucky, in press Spring 2023. "Our Quilts" is included in *Small Acreages* with her permission.

Versions of the following essays, often notably different, have appeared in these publications:

Kentucky Humanities
    "A Tobacco Kind of Christmas"
    "America McGinnis"

"Lilacs and Spirea"

"My Library Room"

"Nat Lee"

"What Books Have Meant to Me"

Kudzu

    "Down Yonder in the Pawpaw Patch"

    (as "Indigenous")

Goode, James B. ed., *Kentucky's Twelve Days of Christmas.* Frankfort:

    Kentucky Monthly, 2012.

    "Shepherds in Bathrobes"

Versions of these essays were included in Stamper's earlier books:

You Can Go Anywhere. Nicholasville, KY: Wind, 2008.

    "Beams"

    "Death of a Farmer" (as "January Rain")

    "Family Reunions"

    "Nat Lee"

    "Shepherds in Bathrobes"

Butter in the Morning. Nicholasville: Wind, 2012.

    "A Tobacco Kind of Christmas"

    "Christmas Eve"

    "Leon Harris"

AUTHOR'S NOTES AND BIBLIOGRAPHY

The English language has ever been in flux even within generations. I have made a sincere effort to honor current preferences regarding racial identity but beg the reader's patience with inconsistencies. Older terminology contained in quoted historical documents is clearly indicated as such by quotation marks.

In my research for "Here on Eagle Creek," I am indebted to Joan Kincaid, Owen County (Kentucky) Clerk, for her assistance in accessing the original copies of the wills and property division documents of Susanah Herndon Rogers and James Herndon (Owen County Kentucky Will Book D.)

For prose effect in the Aunt Sukey section of "Here on Eagle Creek" I list the names of those freed in Rogers's 1838 will. However, my list was informed by comparing it to the more legible names provided in the 1847 division of her property. Readers should be aware that the heirs named in the 1838 will are written in a hand difficult to decipher and with phonetic spelling that varies from the more standardized spelling of the same names in the 1847 property division document.

One name in the Rogers will was not readable to my eye nor was that individual accounted for in the later property division. Two other names in the will are also absent from the property division. It may be presumed that deaths occurred between 1838 and 1847. Also, births likely occurred. Theophilus, for example, has four children mentioned—although not by name—in the 1847 property settlement.

Locust family researchers also should note that only first names are listed in Rogers's 1838 will. However, each emancipated heir carries the surname Locust in the 1847 property division document.

In writing the historical essays, "Here on Eagle Creek" and "Nat Lee," I consulted the following secondary sources:

Bryant, James C. *Mountain Island in Owen County, Kentucky: The Settlers and Their Churches*. Owenton, KY: Owen County Historical Society, 1986.

Ciment, James. Another America: *The Story of Liberia and the Former Slaves Who Ruled It*. NY: Hill & Wang, 2013.

Ficklin, John Herndon & Ann Herndon. Woodford County Marriage Bond, 1791 (image). Kentucky County Marriage Records, 1783–1965. Ancestry.com https://www.ancestry.com/imageviewer/collections/61372/images/TH-1951-30517-12664-74?pId=902449406 (last accessed Jan. 2022.).

Herndon, John G. *The Herndons of Virginia*. Philadelphia: Privately Printed, 1947. Allen County Public Library Genealogy Center https://archive.org/details/herndonfamilyofv1hern (last accessed Jan. 2022.).

Houchens, Mariam Sidebottom. *History of Owen County, Kentucky*. Louisville: Owen County Historical Society, 1976.

Kentucky Life. "Season 11, Episode 6/The Liberian Connection." PBS.org. video, 27m 30s. 5 Feb. 2005. https://www.pbs.org/video/the-liberian-connection-fzibeq/. (last accessed Jan. 2022).

Lindsey, Susan E. *Liberty Brought Us Here*. Lexington: University Press of Kentucky, 2020.

Mansfield, James Roger. *Locust Grove Plantation in Spotsylvania County, Virginia*. Privately published, 1972.

Ranck, George Washington. *The Travelling Church: An Account of the Baptist Exodus From Virginia to Kentucky in 1781 Under the Leadership of Rev. Lewis Craig and Capt. William Ellis: With Historical Notes (1891)*. NJ: Princeton, 1910. https://babel.hathitrust.org/cgi/pt?id=njp.32101062265044&view=1up&seq=1&skin=202 (last accessed Jan. 2022).

Renick, Robert M. *Kentucky Place Names*. Lexington: University Press of Kentucky, 1984.

Snyder, Christina. *Great Crossings: Indians, Settlers & Slaves in the Age of Jackson*. NY: Oxford University Press, 2019.

Spencer, J.H. *A History of Kentucky Baptists* Vol II, 1885. Gallatin, TN: Church History Research & Archive, 1984.

ABOUT THE AUTHOR

GEORGIA GREEN STAMPER, a seventh-generation Kentuckian, grew up in North Central Kentucky on an Owen County tobacco farm that has belonged to one member or another of her family for almost two centuries. Her father was a farmer who loved to read, and her mother was a high school science teacher. Both were keepers of stories, and they instilled an appreciation of local and family history into their only child. The oral tradition of storytelling that thrived not only in her home but also throughout the rural Kentucky culture of her childhood lives on in Stamper's writing. She says that she strives for a written voice which invites her readers "to sit down with her for a spell and talk."

As a young bride, Stamper moved to Ashland, on the far eastern edge of the state, where the mountains of Appalachia meet the industrialized Ohio River valley. These two rich Kentucky cultures—previously unfamiliar to her—would shape her adulthood. She and her husband Ernie would spend their working years in the Ashland area and would raise their three daughters there.

Although writing was her youthful ambition ("don't all English majors want to be authors?" she asks), Stamper did not begin writing seriously until late midlife when, as she recalls, she "finally ran out of excuses not to." She credits her "beginning" to the encouragement that she received from the writing community at Lexington's Carnegie Center for Learning and Literacy. She found additional ongoing support at the Appalachian Writers' Workshop at Hindman Settlement School. In the years since, her work has been published in numerous literary journals and anthologies and it appears regularly as the back-page essay in *Kentucky Humanities. Her earlier books, You Can Go Anywhere* (Wind 2008) and *Butter in the Morning* (Wind 2012), were both jury selected in their respective years of publication for inclusion in the reading series "New Books by Great Kentucky Writers" at Lexington's Carnegie Center.

Stamper has also written the newspaper column Georgia: On My Mind for a local paper since 2004 and has read many of her stories on NPR member station WUKY. Affiliated with the Kentucky Humanities Council, she speaks frequently to groups throughout the state about the importance of preserving local and personal stories.

A graduate of Transylvania University, Stamper is a former high school English and theater teacher. She and Ernie now live in Lexington, where they drive their six grandchildren wherever the children need to go—but, of course, she tells them a family story along the way. *Small Acreages* is her third collection of essays.

Printed in the USA
CPSIA information can be obtained
at www.ICGtesting.com
JSHW020201301023
50818JS00010B/18

9 781945 049255